READING:

A Human Right

and

A Human Problem

RALPH C. STAIGER, University of Delaware
OLIVER ANDRESEN, Chicago State College
Editors

Proceedings of the Second World Congress on Reading
Copenhagen, Denmark
August 1–3, 1968

INTERNATIONAL READING ASSOCIATION
Six Tyre Avenue · Newark, Delaware, U.S.A.

INTERNATIONAL READING ASSOCIATION

OFFICERS

President: LEO FAY, Indiana University, Bloomington, Indiana
President-Elect: HELEN HUUS, University of Missouri, Kansas City, Missouri
Past President: H. ALAN ROBINSON, Hofstra University, Old Westbury, New York

DIRECTORS

Term expiring Spring 1969
MARGARET J. EARLY, Syracuse University, Syracuse, New York
THEODORE HARRIS, University of Puget Sound, Tacoma, Washington
EVE MALMQUIST, National School for Educational Research, Linköping, Sweden

Term expiring Spring 1970
MILLARD H. BLACK, City Unified School District, Los Angeles, California
AMELIA MELNIK, University of Arizona, Tucson, Arizona
VIRGINIA D. YATES, Metropolitan Junior College, Kansas City, Missouri

Term expiring Spring 1971
WILLIAM K. DURR, Michigan State University, East Lansing, Michigan
MILDRED H. FREEMAN, Metropolitan Public Schools, Nashville, Tennessee
ETHEL M. KING, University of Calgary, Calgary, Alberta

Executive Secretary-Treasurer: RALPH C. STAIGER, University of Delaware, Newark, Delaware

Assistant Executive Secretary: RONALD W. MITCHELL, International Reading Association, Newark, Delaware

Publications Coordinator: FAYE R. BRANCA, International Reading Association, Newark, Delaware

Program was arranged by the Second World Congress Committee

Cochairmen

Eve Malmquist, Sweden   Dorothy Kendall Bracken, U.S.A.

Committee Members

H. Alan Robinson, U.S.A.   Mogens Jansen, Denmark
Marion Jenkinson, Canada   Joyce M. Morris, England
Helen M. Robinson, U.S.A.

Foreword

On August 8 and 9, 1966, the First World Congress on Reading, sponsored by IRA, was held in Paris. Five hundred educators from sixteen countries were in attendance. The proceedings of that Congress, *Reading Instruction: An International Forum,* was published by IRA in 1967.

On August 1, 2, and 3, 1968, the Second World Congress on Reading was held in Copenhagen, cosponsored by the Danish National Association of Reading Teachers and the International Reading Association. About thirteen hundred educators from twenty-five countries were in attendance. The present volume is the proceedings of the Second World Congress.

This publication does not contain all papers presented in Copenhagen nor does it reflect fully the stimulating dialogues, formal and informal, carried on among the participants. A complete list of program participants appears at the end of this volume. The provocative papers included here, however, provide some of the flavor of the Congress — the fresh ideas and knowledge about reading instruction revealed by conferees from countries throughout the world.

Although you will find all papers of great interest, I should like to direct attention particularly to the opening papers by Eve Malmquist and Arthur I. Gates for, in addition to insightful and thought-provoking content, they relate to two significant events which took place during the Congress. Eve Malmquist's keynote address on the theme of the Congress served as the basic material for a series of resolutions concerned with world literacy which were drafted by an international committee and were received with acclaim by the total body of participants at the Congress. It is anticipated that, growing from these resolutions, an international group of leaders will form a steering committee to begin a worldwide campaign for the eradication of illiteracy. Arthur Gates' paper is an award response. Dr. Gates was selected by an international group to become the recipient of the first World Congress in Reading Award for his distinguished service and many contributions to a better understanding of the reading process and to reading instruction throughout the world.

Another important occurrence reported at the Congress, but not included in the body of this volume, will be of interest to you. The International Reading Association was one of five groups to be awarded honorable mention for the Mohammad Reza Pahlavi Prize for meritorious work in adult literacy. The award was made possible through the generous gift of H.I.M. the Shahinshah of Iran and was awarded by a jury appointed by the Director-General of UNESCO.

The success of the Second World Congress was due to the concerted efforts of many people and organizations. Eve Malmquist initiated the idea of a Scandinavian congress and helped with concepts and details from start to finish. Ralph Staiger and the IRA headquarters staff worked long hours in implementing and arranging the congress plan. Dorothy Kendall Bracken was mainly responsible for making the congress plan operational and spent many long hours revamping and revising the program. Thanks are also due to other members of the Second World Congress who provided significant ideas, suggested possible participants, and helped in shaping the program.

Special gratitude must be offered to Mogens Jansen, member of the Second World Congress Committee and Local Arrangements Chairman in Copenhagen. Dr. Jansen, along with many Scandinavian educators and the Danish International Students' Congress Service, was responsible for the smooth and professional operation of the Congress.

H. ALAN ROBINSON, *President*
International Reading Association
1967—1968

Introduction

The reading process has no boundaries. Through reading, literate people can learn the thinking, not only of their own people, but that of other nations as well. Certainly, therefore, reading is a process through which mankind can find universal understanding. The Second World Congress on Reading in Copenhagen was a step towards this ideal.

Although the people of the world speak in many tongues, the reading of these written languages has much in common. Consequently, the reading instruction in one land has problems in common with such instruction in any other country. At the IRA congress researchers and educators discussed the common problems and shared suggested answers which might be found fruitful for the teaching of reading in widely different cultures and localities.

Many of the papers presented are included in this book. In addition to the keynote address and the award response, presentations range from a discussion of how successful readers have learned, by Ruth Strang, to the very specific discussion of children's literature from many lands, by IRA President-elect Helen Huus.

The papers presented in the Scandinavian languages will appear in the *Skandinavisk Tidskrift för Läspedagoger.* Some of the other presentations by their nature did not lend themselves to formal papers and were not submitted. Since final plans for publication were not completed until November 1968, certain of the Congress papers have appeared in professional journals and, therefore, have not been included here. A complete list of program participants appears at the end of this volume.

The purpose of publication, of course, is to allow for a vast extension of the profitable pooling of ideas at Copenhagen. Through such international conferences and their resulting proceedings, a more lucid appreciation of the reading process and the enhancement of reading instruction can be gained by inquiring educators throughout the world.

RALPH C. STAIGER
OLIVER ANDRESEN
Editors

Contents

Eve Malmquist

NATIONAL SCHOOL FOR EDUCATIONAL RESEARCH
LINKÖPING, SWEDEN

Reading: A Human Right and a Human Problem

"Everyone has the right to education." This demand for education as a human right was proclaimed in 1948 by the General Assembly of the United Nations in one of the articles within its universal "Declaration of Human Rights". This article further reads: "Education shall be free, at least in the elementary and fundamental stages. Elementary education shall be compulsory. Technical and professional education shall be made generally available, and higher education shall be equally accessible to all on the basis of merit".

It seems natural and quite justifiable that we now, twenty years later, in 1968, the proclaimed International Year of Human Rights, try to form some kind of opinion as to what extent these claims on equality of educational opportunity for all have been fulfilled. One of the most significant features of the past twenty years is the enormous and rapidly rising demand for education in all countries around the world. The right of the individual to be given the opportunity to develop fully his potential abilities has in principle been generally recognized. However, in practice this ideal seems extremely far from being universally achieved.

Over 50 per cent illiteracy in 62 of the member countries of U. N.

The latest information by UNESCO shows that 50 percent of the world's children of primary and secondary school age are not going to school at all. More than 40 percent of the world's adult population — about 800 million — is estimated to be unable to read and write. At least 65 percent of the world's population is estimated to fall below the level of functional literacy, when the criterion of fourth grade level of reading ability is used.

A few other examples might be appropriate: 1) of five and one-half million inhabitants in Algeria over fifteen years of age, four million — nearly 80 percent — are illiterates; 2) with only 24 percent of the population of India being literate, this percentage means that in a population of about 435 mil-

1

lion, 330 million are illiterates and, consequently, need to be taught reading skills of an elementary kind; 3) only 5 percent of the entire population of Ethiopia is able to read; 4) the illiteracy rate is estimated to be over 50 percent in sixtytwo of the member countries of United Nations; 5) in twenty countries more than 90 percent of the population is unable to read and write; 6) in many countries the female population is almost entirely illiterate; 7) and what might be even more shocking, as many as eight countries in Europe report a rate of illiteracy ranging from 10 percent to 65 percent of the population at the age of fifteen and above.

Despite all our previous efforts we are faced with a very disquieting picture at present. The number of adult illiterates, rather than being on the decline, is actually increasing at the rate of twenty-five to thirty million persons a year! This distressing fact is attributed to the circumstance that the educational progress, though considerable, has not been enough to keep pace with the rapid population growth.

Reading ability necessary for survival in our world of today

The person living in the twentieth century who has not been given the opportunity to learn to read cannot function in a proper way, cannot live a full human, individual, and social life. He is deprived of a fundamental human right to gain further education, to gain access to one of the most invaluable instruments for learning. It has been said: "Learning is living and living is learning". In a real sense, therefore, the ability to read is an indispensable element in a person's equipment for living in every corner of the world of today.

Recently, an Indian delegate at a UNESCO conference spoke on this subject in the following terms: "Being without reading ability, half of the population of the world has no possibility to realize the human rights. They will remain unaware of the opportunities science and technology give us to fight hunger, poverty, and diseases. They will also be excluded from the common cultural heritage which is laid down in written documents".

Illiteracy has always existed. Yet today it has grown to be a really acute problem of all mankind. In the primitive society with its traditional pattern of living, inability to read was hardly a big handicap for the fulfillment of a human life. But today enormously improved means of transportation and communication have brought peoples living in all corners of this earth closer and closer together. The use of the results of technical development has been more and more necessary for survival everywhere and, therefore, illiteracy has become an increasingly serious problem. There will be fewer and fewer jobs available for unskilled illiterate workers in any part of our technical civilization of today.

After the second world war many new self-governing countries were established and, consequently, a new world situation was created. Democracy in our sense cannot be maintained in a society where the citizens are not even able to read the ballot form. Therefore, a strong political demand for universal literacy is emerging. The rapidly growing gap between low income countries — and the map of those poor countries is to a great extent identical with the countries which recently have acquired national independence and which have a very high illitteracy percentage — and the high income countries has become an extremely actual and ever-growing economic and political danger in the world of today.

If we want to conquer poverty, hunger, and disease in the world, we have to conquer illiteracy first. Illiteracy is the most serious handicap for economic, political, social, and individual development that we know. In fact, illiteracy is becoming more generally recognized as the most irreconcilable hindrance to development and progress everywhere in the world and, furthermore, as a grave block to international understanding and cooperation. Illiteracy is regarded as one of the subtlest but most stubborn threats to peace in the world today because it divides nations within themselves and among one another into two groups — the literates and the illiterates.

U Thant: "An invitation to violence"

People in the advanced industrialized countries must realize that their future welfare and security are dependent upon the prosperity of the developing countries. This fact was emphasized by U. Thant, General Secretary of the United Nations, at the opening session of the United Nations Economic and Social Council (ECOSOC) in Geneva. He also expressed the opinion that a failure to diminish the gap between the rich and the poor countries of the world "is an invitation to violence". Differences of political organization appear to be less significant and less of an obstacle to cooperation than it was formerly supposed. As Richard Goodings and Joseph Lauwerys have expressed it: "The only differences of any importance are not those between the communist and the capitalist, but those between the hungry and the affluent, between the educated and the illiterate".

To an increasing extent the whole world's problems concern all of us. We can no longer ignore the problems of those who live in another part of the country nor the problems of those who live in another nation or on another continent. We have to face the problems, to share them, and to seek solutions for them on a worldwide basis.

Many important regional meetings have been held under the auspices of UNESCO in this decade.

"A selective stategy" is now used by UNESCO

What has been characterized as a turning point in the whole struggle against illiteracy was the UNESCO-sponsored World Congress of Ministers of Education for the Eradication of Illiteracy in Teheran, 1965. According to the recommendations of this congress, accepted by the General Assembly of the United Nations, a new approach to the problem is now being tried by UNESCO. "A selective strategy — a strategy of intensive projects rather than of extensive campaigns —" is used on an experimental basis. At the present time special attention has been given to a small number of countries — Algeria, Iran, Mali, Tanzania, and Ecuador.

Instead of attempting to teach everyone in these countries to read and write, UNESCO has selected certain sections of society, such as industrialized and agricultural areas, where strong motives for learning could be expected by the foreseeable use of reading ability to raise the standard of living. It has been emphasized that literacy should not be regarded as an end in itself nor as a problem to be solved in isolation. Literacy should be regarded as a first essential step in a life of continuing education, in which reading ability is an indispensable tool. Literate workers in industry and agriculture are assumed to be able to take advantage of the ongoing professional training much easier and quicker than illiterate workers and, thereby, to pave the way for an increased productivity. By increased production, better profits and hopefully higher salaries will follow and, in that way, consumption and demand should increase. These results, in turn, should bring about an acceleration of the economic process. Then the "evil circle" in a developing country should be broken. The results of these experiments will be analyzed and evaluated during the years 1969 and 1970, and the experiences gained will be the basis for enlarged literacy campaigns later on.

Many signs suggest that governments as well as individuals in practically all nations around the world are awakening to the presence of illiteracy. And it is not one day too soon.

But when it comes to deeds so many difficulties and so many delicate priority-order problems emerge, that the effect of adult literacy programs so far has been much less than was expected. The problems are, therefore, growing and turning out to be even more overwhelming than before. Admirable work has been accomplished, but much, much more remains to be done before the goal of a universal literacy is achieved.

There is certainly a need for drastic action to eradicate illiteracy once and for all as some national representatives have pointed out at the General Assembly of the United Nations. Many leaders in various countries, however, have turned away the declaration of the fundamental human right to education — if not in words, at least in practical action — and, therefore, have postponed the realisation of the goal of a universal literacy to a future generation, to the years of 2010 to 2020.

We must raise our aims as to functional literacy

From my point of view, the struggle against illiteracy is one of the most important and also one of the most gigantic and demanding tasks of our present generation. This task has, as I see it, two facets: first, we must eliminate illiteracy and, second, we must raise the standard of functional literacy.

The technological revolution, which promises to affect within a few years all parts of the earth, may force us to raise our sights about functional literacy. We no longer can be content with a fourth-grade standard of reading ability. In my view this standard needs to be raised at least to a ninth-grade level. In many highly industrialized countries, workers will by 1980 need a reading capacity of even a twelfth-grade level in order to comprehend effectively instructions and blueprints. But, to repeat, at least a ninth-grade reading proficiency will be required.

We can anticipate that, because of rapid rate of change, those children who this year, 1968, enter the first-grade of the elementary schools throughout the world and whose professional, productive, mature lives will span the years of — let us say — 1980 to 2040, will have to make at least three or four changes in occupation.

The heavy flow of extensive data and information from computers will create reading problems of great significance for people in the world of tomorrow. Without proper training in making intelligent decisions as to the exact kind of information needed, and in the ability to do rapid selective reading, they will drown in the informational deluge.

What would it cost, minimally, to teach people around the world to read? Is it at all economically feasible? As given by UNESCO the cost of making *one* person literate varies from $5.25 to $7.50. Yes, that is all — $5.25 to $7.50 per person depending upon the region concerned. To teach 800 million people to read and write would, therefore, cost around 5,800 million dollars. To this amount we should add the costs of follow-up campaigns for the stimulation of continued reading and for the production and distribution of books meeting the aspirations and the daily needs of the readers. These costs might raise the sum needed from nine to ten billion dollars or more. Huge sums of money, indeed, but as a comparison I may mention that approximately 150 billion dollars a year are allotted to defense by the various countries of the world — fifteen times as much as needed for a world literacy campaign.

Under the circumstances, we have to face the fact that a variety of sources must be explored and tapped to meet the enormous needs. It is unrealistic to expect the United Nations to provide these sums and to hire the hundreds of thousands of teachers and experts who will be needed to teach and to produce instruments and materials for such a worldwide literacy campaign.

World Literacy Day — September 8, 1970 — a starting point for the campaign

May I share with you a plan of action and some fund-raising ideas which have occurred to me in this connection? You may remember that the World Congress in Teheran in 1965 recommended that September 8 should be annually proclaimed World Literacy Day. This suggestion strikes me as an excellent idea. As I see it, the propaganda value of such a day has not been very extensively used. I would like to suggest that this day, World Literacy Day, September 8 of 1970, be employed as the starting point for an information campaign, a promotional campaign for the eradication of illiteracy throughout the world.

Further, I would like to propose that the best available public relations experts from all over the world be consulted to make this goal a reality. Effective and imaginative use of every mass communication medium should be made — films, radio, television, newspapers, magazines, pamphlets, or posters. The services of artists, actors, and others should be brought to bear on this global drive with cooperation across all national and regional boundaries on many areas. Such a concentrated information campaign should draw on organizations and individuals from all over the world for aid, not only in finances but also in expert teaching and in the creating of books and other teaching materials.

In addition, I would like to propose that this present World Congress on Reading in Copenhagen go on record as expressing its support of the resolution by the Teheran Congress in 1965 and as recommending a transfer from words to deeds, from theories to action, in an intensification of the efforts to eradicate illiteracy, effectively, in all countries of the earth.

Though UNESCO should evidently take the lead in this venture, I think the IRA should offer its expertise for the teaching of reading. The cooperation of other international specialized agencies should be elicited — agencies such as FAO, WHO, UNICEF, and the like — in order to make possible food for development campaigns and health campaigns parallel to the literacy campaign. If you are starving and sick, you cannot work efficiently nor enjoy learning to read. By the year of 1970 we should have on hand findings from experimental reading projects carried on by UNESCO to selected groups in Algeria, Mali, and other countries. Also, 1970 has been designated International Education Year. Would not September 8, 1970, be an effective starting date for the launching of the massive worldwide teaching campaign?

To finance the teaching campaign, funds will have to be found to supplement the annual contributions from UNESCO and the United Nations' Special Fund.

Suggestions for financing a World Literacy Campaign

I have the following suggestions to make in this connection:

1. That in 1970, one-half percent of the respective budgets of all countries of the world be allocated to this World Literacy Campaign.
2. That in 1970 each nation will advance to the disposal of this campaign one percent of its elementary school teachers, for a limited three-months period of service, to serve in the capacity of teachers or as consultants to groups of teachers in the countries concerned.
3. That the following institutions be asked to donate the total income of the eighth of September 1970 to the Worldwide Literacy Campaign:
   a. All companies producing and publishing books.
   b. All newspapers and magazines.
   c. All firms connected with the communication business, such as television and radio companies, news, magazines, newspapers, and advertising agencies.
   d. All producers of teaching materials of various kinds, including manufacturers of television sets, radio receivers, radio transmitters, and the like.

The role of IRA's reading experts in the Campaign

What part would you see yourselves playing, you experts in psychology and methodology of reading? I see you as being particularly qualified to serve as leaders and resource persons in a variety of capacities. For instance:

1. By virtue of your knowledge within the reading field and your national authority in these matters, you are in a unique position to activate your government to contribute to such a world literacy campaign (not only for citizens within your own country but for all illiterates around the world).
2. You are in a position to organize, stimulate, and help authorities in the training of teachers for service in the developing countries.
3. You are in a position to assist in the work of constructing and testing reading materials for use in the teaching of children and of adults in various countries.
4. You are in a position to assist in the work of preparing manuals for local teachers in developing countries as well as to assist in setting up radio and television programs on the teaching of reading.

5. And finally, would you not be in a position of being able to appeal to teachers' organizations in the developed countries to recommend urgently that each individual teacher donate his whole day's income for Literacy Day, September 8, 1970, to a world literacy campaign?

You will surely have a great number of proposals and suggestions to add to these which have occurred to me. I am of the view that all of you, assembled here today, are, as I am, both emotionally and intellectually struck by the extraordinary urgency and by the great magnitude of the problem of illiteracy in the world today. Also I trust that many of you are willing to devote the best of your efforts to assist in proceeding to solutions to this farreaching, yes, this global problem. Actually, this is a very exciting venture, one full of challenge and promise, leading to the release of so much human potential.

By taking the initiative to such a joint action, by giving guiding principles for programs of various kinds and at different levels, IRA can make an enormously important contribution to the fulfillment of one of its main purposes: "to improve reading ability among all peoples around the world".

From my point of view, we have to realize that we cannot afford to wait for the next generation to solve the problem of illiteracy. It has to be attacked and solved within a reasonable time in our generation. The time to plan and carry through this gigantic concerted operation in solving a problem of a worldwide common concern — "the shame and scandal of illiteracy", as Director General of UNESCO, René Maheu, has called it — is not in 1980 or in 2015 — IT IS RIGHT NOW!

ARTHUR I. GATES

PROFESSOR EMERITUS
TEACHERS COLLEGE, COLUMBIA UNIVERSITY
NEW YORK, NEW YORK
UNITED STATES OF AMERICA

Reflection and Return

AS I MOVE AROUND IN VARIOUS circles, I hear repeatedly the voice of conviction that we are now in or entering a professional revolution. I have heard this same voice on several occasions during my life, and I think it spoke truly. I feel that some of our most illustrious advances have occurred when we became fully aware of and deeply involved as educators in such revolutions. The one we are in now may have far-reaching effects upon the role of reading and the other language arts both in school and society. We must resist the temptation to disregard this revolution.

In many sections of the United States, economic and social subdivisions of society have developed so separately and so differently that the pride of our professional past, the school as the national "melting pot", the single "common school", is being severely attacked at all levels. At the upper levels, the students themselves are leading the rebellion; at the elementary and intermediate educational levels, the parents are heavily engaged. The typical American reading program seems now clearly to be unsuitable for large blocks of children in such ghettos as New York City's Harlem, in sections of some of our rural localities, and in other communities. Our most highly trained and experienced teachers of reading are finding to their dismay that they are ill equipped to deal with the youngsters in these areas. Indeed, Teachers College's specialist in these minority groups, Ianni, recently wrote, "Many are questioning whether schools — at least as we know them — will long continue to exist in these areas". They are in fact being rejected in sections of New York City right now. Probably nothing less than thorough reorganization of materials, methods, and objectives, perhaps on a worldwide scale, will meet the demands of the social, political, and general educational upheaval now sweeping around the globe.

The effectiveness of every phase of education is dependent upon the conditions of life in general at the time. Neither the general patterns nor particular materials nor methods of teaching are independent absolutes. No educational patterns or practices and no materials or types of communication can safely be regarded as absolutely right or wrong, as relatively good or bad, for all communities, or schools or teachers or curricula, for all social or economic or intellectual groups or individuals, or for all times. Adaptation to a wider variety of conditions and societies and at more frequent intervals than we have heretofore attempted should be our practice in the future.

Many changes now under way may have worldwide influence on reading and learning to read. One, for example, is the recent appearance of very inexpensive, tiny transistor radios which are rapidly becoming the possession of large numbers of persons of all ages, all over the earth, in all walks of life — isolated shepherds, fishermen, farmers, and lumbermen and all manner of children, teenagers and adults, whether laborer or loafer in every kind of town and city. Several scholars have asserted recently that these tiny radios have become the most powerful means of communication now available to leaders, especially political leaders in many different countries, notably in nations in which a large proportion of the population is unable to read. These radios are perfect instruments for propaganda, good or bad. Their use, likely soon to be universal, raises many questions relating to the educational possibilities and effects of a new, very convenient auditory, as contrasted with visual, approach. It raises problems that are worldwide in nature and should be studied on a worldwide scale.

At the same time a new wind has appeared which tends to bend the willow in the opposite direction. In presenting this development, I have yielded to the temptation to quote from an article of mine published in 1928. "Learning to read (differs) from learning to understand spoken language only in one respect: in the former a complex visual stimulus must be recognized and associated with some object, event, situation, or quality; in the latter a complex auditory stimulus is reacted to similarly. In the one case we interpret auditory words; in the other, visual . . . There is no evidence to my knowledge that the visual forms (are) intrinsically more difficult; indeed, they may be easier" (p. 4—5). I repeat now as I said then that children learn to read spoken words before written or printed ones not because it is easier or more natural but only because they can be presented to children so much more easily and, therefore, more often. The spoken word can wing its way around curves and corners and through solid walls in a way that printed words cannot.

When I presented this idea more than forty years ago, it was usually dismissed as the wisecrack of a typical young crackpot professor. But the evidence suggests that it is theoretically sound and practically demonstrable. I have taught without difficulty many one-year-old infants to read quite a few printed words. Congenital deaf-mutes can learn to recognize printed words quite readily. It was found recently that in areas where there are many television programs and where most children have television sets in their homes, youngsters from two to five years of age spent an average of more than forty-five hours a week before them, not only hearing audible but seeing visible words. And large numbers of these children are learning to read early as well as to listen to words. Walter MacGinitie and I found in a survey of representative American children, from the rural and remote areas as well as the urban, that even now approximately eighty percent are able to read from a few to a great many words before they enter school. Forty years ago, I found the proportion to be only about ten percent.

Only a little ingenuity is required to develop television programs and related materials, such as little booklets in printed form, to induce the very young to learn to read by themselves in the home quite as they now learn to understand spoken words. Indeed, several programs of this sort are soon to be tried out. Television sets, like radios, are becoming cheaper, smaller, and more foolproof. They may rapidly become as widely used as transistor radios.

Now that the infantile eye as well as the ear in all parts of the world may soon be attracted to words, what are we to do about the staggering possibilities of educating the new generation of youngsters before as well as after their sixth birthday? Shall we emphasize visual reading more or less in comparison with oral listening? The answer will doubtless vary among different cultures and communities. We must, therefore, discover the crucial considerations. Here is a charming little problem which you experts on all the language arts are in the best position to tackle, a problem in which a worldwide attack seems likely to be desirable.

Two views of the importance of studying practices in other lands have been widely held in the past. One is the old idea that the study of education in a foreign culture is often not very fruitful because conditions are so different; findings, it is alleged, are shrouded by the mists of so many uncontrolled variations that local applications are hazardous. One had better work nearer to home. I fear that I was restrained at times by such a thought. I did so even, in my earlier years, while I was conducting what I now regard as my most significant studies — studies which should have revealed my error. These were a number of my earliest investigations of what I felt represented critically distinctive cases, such as children who had been deaf from birth, weak or markedly acute in visual and auditory discrimination, left-eyed or left-handed, or otherwise exceptional. Only recently has it come to me with a shock that in choosing these subjects as the best of my humble efforts, I was admitting the high value one should place on studies of children with equally conspicuous differences due to living in different lands, learning different native languages, and adjusting to divergent early social, personal, and parental characteristics. The mists produced by different conditions must be cleared away to reveal the basic principles. All I can say today is that I have at long last been cured of this ancient blindness. Moreover, I now believe that of all the teachable activities, the language arts are foremost in the extent to which the light from other lands will increase the clearness of one's vision at home.

Since the language arts are so greatly and often so subtly influenced by almost every aspect of everyday life, high competence in all phases of life is needed to formulate the best practical plans. In trying to improve education in the language arts we must, therefore, recognize the acute need for more help and information than we have been accustomed to from fields such as sociology, social anthropology, health, economics, biochemistry, clinical psychology, psychiatry, medicine, linguistics, politics, business, and many others.

Compared to many fields, we have been overly cautious and preoccupied often with minor details of a practice when we should have been challenging the whole structure. We must be careful lest we become visited by a Plague of Pettiness. We must develop the type of fearlessness shown, for example, in medicine and surgery. We have been slow to grasp the advantages offered by technical devices and experimental apparatus, computers in diagnosis and management, and mechanical aids in teaching. It is high time for us to shift from the most conservative to the most progressive — yes, even the most venturesome — of all the professional groups. Let us not hesitate longer to do the equivalent of open heart surgery or heart transplantation in our area.

Like others of those who, in America at least, are called "Senior Citizens", I tend to reflect upon the factors that led me into training concerned with scientific and scholarly study. My first vocational decision was perhaps my most critical one. Shortly before I was graduated from high school, I was presented with two attractive offers — one, a small scholarship to help me attend the University of California and the other, a much larger amount to become a professional baseball player. A few years ago, a former college roommate of mine, a witty wag, commenting on my choice said, "Well, it seems to me that baseball has gotten along better without you than education has with you!"

During my final year as a graduate student, I served as assistant in experimental psychology to J. McKeen Cattell at Columbia University. Cattell was, in important respects, the father of the laboratory experimental psychological study of reading as a result of his brilliant work in Wundt's laboratory in Leipzig. Cattell was also the man who introduced to Thorndike and others in America the statistical method, which he studied under Galton in England after leaving Leipzig. As was true of many other students at that time, I did not go abroad to study psychology mainly because Cattell and others of his generation brought England and the Continent to the United States.

Most of my earliest contacts with psychology were European in flavor. My first student textbook was Wundt's *Human and Animal Psychology*. Bernheim's *Suggestive Therapeutics,* an early statement of typical French abnormal psychology, and Binet's reports were among my first readings. I struggled with the mental chemistry of Titchener and other early English psychologists. I laboriously translated from German the three large volumes of "Lectures" on educational psychology by Meumann.

During my last year as a student I carried forward under Thorndike and Cattell the study of the group or mass-statistical approach which I had previously undertaken at Berkeley on my own. But at the time I took up quarters in Teachers College under Thorndike, my first love was the analytical, experimental, and theoretical psychology in which I had taken my doctorate under Cattell and Woodworth. For at least a dozen years thereafter, I used these approaches as my primary ones. A technique I used frequently was to gather data from two or more comparable groups of subjects pursuing two or more experimental programs and subject all of them before, during, and after the experience to intensive individual study by means of various tests, experimental devices, and intensive observation. Indeed, I now view this combination of group and intensive individual study as the most rewarding that I have ever used.

But as time went on, I shifted more and more to the mass-statistical approach as most of my American contemporaries were doing. The causes of this change seem quite clear to me. The analytical-experimental approach proved to be relatively slow and uncertain. By contrast, a group study could be carried out by having a few before-and-after tests given by student assistants, by turning on the computing machines, and reading the results — results that could be obtained by a "researcher" who had not seen a single one of his "experimental" subjects.

As some of you know, I have been expressing my deep concern about our shift in America from the laborious analytical experimental studies to group methods to the point where the former have almost become extinct. This trend is tragic. If I appear to be extremely critical of mass study, I do so only because so many persons in education seemed to believe that it is an adequate substitute for the more analytical experimental attack. It is not. Its value is great for many purposes, but its limitations for many of our most vital problems are conspicuous. The crucial fact to remember is that the pattern of abilities and other characteristics in an individual is not the same as the pattern in a group. An error in some minds is the idea that an individual is a sort of miniature of the average of a group. Most of the leaders in scholarly study in such wonderfully productive fields as biochemistry, metallurgy, agriculture, and especially in our closest kin among the profession, medicine, are clearly aware of these distinctions. If you have any doubts on this point, please read Selye's splendid book, *From Dream to Discovery: On Being A Scientist* (New York: McGraw-Hill, 1964). Nearly every word in this fine volume by Selye, probably the most insightful authority on biological science in the world today, has meaning for scholars in education and related areas. Selye, for some time the head of a medical research institute in Canada, is Viennese by birth and education.

These details of my professional life and convictions suggest the main point of my title. After prolonged reflection I have reached the conclusion that if I had assurance of many vigorous years before me, I would happily return, somewhat in the fashion of the prodigal son, to my adopted teacher-parents at whose knees I learned primarily the analytical-experimental, the old-world approaches. I would certainly revive my concern with the worldwide professional scene which was more adequate long ago than it is now. Had I returned years ago, I would have become a better scholar. At any rate, I am now confident that the energy and generosity of this worldwide organization will become for others as it has for me the source of a clearer awareness of the sources of a more fruitful professional enterprise during the next generation.

Lest these comments and those of many other critics, both qualified and unqualified, during recent years cause doubt that scientific study can contribute richly to the improvement of teaching of the language arts, reflect for a moment on the fact that we have had a trifling amount of such research in comparison with many other fields, such as medicine, agriculture, and mechanical engineering. Educational research has lived on crumbs during my days, but I believe that it is soon to join other groups at the table. Indeed, it has already had at least a few substantial handouts. For example, in several recent instances the amount of money made available for *each* of a few short-time (two- to five-year) investigations has been greater than the amount I received for all the research work I have carried out during my entire lifetime. If some of those of our groups now show signs of getting indigestion from the unaccustomed feast at the main table, we need not worry. They will soon get adjusted to a rich diet. In the long run, a bountiful table for scholarly and scientific study will provide much that we need to give full vigor to our profession.

Ruth Strang

ONTARIO INSTITUTE FOR STUDIES IN EDUCATION
TORONTO, ONTARIO, CANADA

How Successful Readers Learn: A Global View

From an international viewpoint, reading is the key to communication and contributes to the solution of world problems of poverty and animosity. From a personal viewpoint, reading is the key to continuing education, employment, and enjoyment. These goals may be achieved through effective teaching of reading.

Previous international conferences have explored many aspects of the psychology of teaching reading. There are two aspects, however, that I should like to emphasize. The first is learning about the reading process from the reader himself. The second is an integration of aims, learning process, and teaching procedures.

We have gained understanding of the learning process from animal experimentation, laboratory experiments with children, and research carried out under natural school conditions. Some important research on the reading process has used introspective-retrospective verbalization as the main method of collecting data. To learn how a child learns, we need to get close to the child, not to be aloof like the psychologist who stumbled over a child and exclaimed, "Oh, my goodness, what is that!" We need to acquire Piaget's genius for getting into the child's mind — into his thinking and feeling, (Inhelder and Piaget, 1958).

The most important source of understanding of why and how children learn to read has been neglected, namely, the day-by-day study of children as an intrinsic part of teaching.

Although we have learned much from studies of why children fail in reading, we could learn still more from intensive study of why and how children of different abilities and backgrounds achieve their reading potentialities.

Retrospective Reports

When successful readers were asked, "How did you learn to read so well?" some said, "I don't know; I just did". Others spoke of "sounding out" the word by letters or by syllables. Still others remembered that their mothers had taught them words printed on cards. Quite a few learned by asking someone to tell them words that they saw on signs, boxes, or in books. They seemed to be aware of the interaction or interplay of oral language and meanings. Many mentioned hearing someone read aloud to them while they looked at the pictures and print on each page. There were also a number of idiosyncratic recollections.

Reports of research and case studies likewise describe diverse methods by which individuals learn to read. A seventeen-year-old boy with an IQ of around 50 reached a reading level of almost third grade after two years of individual instruction using signs, notices, directions, and the Hegge, Kirk, and Kirk (1940) phonic drills as reading materials. Another nonreader, using selections from the Science Research Associates Laboratories and rewarded for his correct responses by tokens of money value, achieved a 4.3 grade level of achievement. Some groups of exceptional children learned in an accepting classroom atmosphere freed from failure, while others responded to pressure methods. Still others learned through a series of programed lessons, the progressive choice method, a kinesthetic and auditory emphasis, the Montessorri method, the initial teaching alphabet, or linguistic readers. One of the main conclusions of the United States Office of Education's extensive first grade studies was that there was no *one* best method of teaching reading.

In pronouncing unfamiliar words, children also use many different methods such as the following.

Singing: "I knew 'sing' and 'ing' and I put them together."
Bring: "I knew 'sing' and put the 'br'sound in place of 's'."
Seem: "I knew that word by the two 'e's' together."
Bark: "I sounded the 'b' and it was with 'a' and 'r' and ends in 'k'."
Pail: "It has two vowels together, so the 'a' is long and the 'i' is silent."
Oswald: (A name in the title of a story) "I saw it in the newspaper. He killed the President."

These are a few examples of word recognition methods used by a single class of first grade children. Included in their learning repertory were variations of structural analysis, phonics, letter naming, consonant substitutions, recognition of unique visual configurations, application of phonic rules or generalizations, and recognition of the word as a whole.

A similar diversity of associations was apparent in twelve- and thirteen-year-olds' retrospective reports of how they had learned the meanings of certain words. Among these associations were out-of-school experiences; dramatization of word meanings; teacher's explanations; associations with people, e.g., *pessimist,* "My grandmother is a pessimist, she has the habit of saying everything bad is going to happen"; and association with things, e.g., *tranquil* with the familiar tranquilizers. Some gained meaning from auditory and visual similarities and contrasts, and in many other diverse and roundabout ways. Such reports give insight into the child's thinking, his ability to express his thoughts, and his understanding of the spoken or written words of others. Introspective-retrospective verbalization also shows the interaction of thinking and feeling and the role of personal relationships in successful reading. In their reading autobiographies, pupils seldom recalled any *specific instruction* in reading that the teacher had given them. We may infer that the teacher had actually given them little help in *how* to read or that the instruction had made little impression on the children. Nor did the pupils associate television with success in reading. If television did contribute to these children's reading proficiency, they apparently were unaware of its value ... at least it was not uppermost in their minds.

These retrospective reports, uninfluenced by leading questions or suggestive checklist statements, give us a glimpse of the manifold ways in which children perceive the process of reading. Retrospective reports are the basis for curriculum planning and teaching; they are useful to appraise the effect of any sequence of instruction and of certain aspects of children's reading achievement. For example, can children explore sound-letter relations and also get meaning from exposure to the complexity of a whole passage?

The second strategy is to relate behavioral objectives and prerequisites to success in reading, to the learning process, and to teaching procedures.

Analysis of the Integration of Aims, Learning Process, and Teaching Procedures

Both the children's responses and pedagogical research on factors associated with children's development in the language arts indicate that the teaching of the communication arts should be concerned with the totality of the task, not only with the separate parts. It should relate the three main aspects: to state definitely the behavioral objectives, analyze each of these tasks, and describe the teaching procedures that would facilitate accomplishment of these tasks.

In this global view of reading we first focus our attention on the specific, definite behavior or competencies to be acquired. These are usually presented as a hierarchy or a sequence. They may be more accurately viewed as a matrix in which mature reading ability develops. At the base of this model is the individual's innate capacity which interacts with physical, intellectual, and social environmental influences. These guide the course of the child's intellectual as well as his physical development. Out of this interaction, the prerequisites for reading develop: cognitive abilities; language and speech; visual and auditory perception, discrimination, memory, sequencing, and integration (Kirk and McCarthy, 1968).

More pervasive in their influence on learning are an openness to experiences and motivation to learn. These psycholinguistic, mental, and emotional prerequisites contribute to the development of sight vocabulary and word recognition skills, which are the foundation for exact comprehension of sentences, paragraphs, and longer passages which, in turn, make possible interpretive, critical, reflective, and creative reading. Accompanying comprehension are the appropriate feeling responses and applications to personal and social development.

For practical purposes, each of these major aspects must be broken down into concrete behavioral objectives, such as being able to identify, discriminate, and recall the consonant sounds in words or the ability to locate and interpret clues of character in literature. This sequential list of specific behavioral objectives serves as a guide to teachers in both a developmental and remedial program. The child starts at, or a little below, the point of competence which he has already acquired.

The next step is to analyze the processes by which these competencies are acquired. This is the process of "task analysis", moving from the concrete to the abstract . . . and from the simple to the complex. Too often we expect a child to achieve higher levels of skills without having mastered the preliminary steps. Too often we ask a child to "get the thought of the paragraph" without giving him any instruction in how to do it. By analysing each task, as in programed learning, we provide progression in his learning experience, leading to success and self-confidence.

For example, the process of deriving meaning from the flow of words in sentences is still relatively unexplored. McCullough (1968) has shown how the reader must constantly refer forward and back in a sentence or paragraph for the meaning of one word after another. I. A. Richards (1968) has described this thought process as feedback leading to "feed forward", the response made to one part of the sentence which leads to anticipation of or clues to the thought ahead. In this process recognition, recall, inference, evaluation, appreciation, and application are all involved.

Certain principles or strategies of learning influence this total program and affect the process at every stage.

Our teaching procedures should stem from the learning process. With a basic understanding of the reading process and how reading competencies are learned, the teacher plans experiences that facilitate children's learning. He provides experiences, gives instruction as needed, selects and analyzes the reading material, responds appropriately, and encourages the practice which the class as a whole, and the individual child as well, needs. The teacher directs his attention first to the child — his abilities, attitudes, interests, and background. He attempts to match the learning situation to the abilities of the child at the moment. The child responds; the teacher reinforces the desired response with recognition or approval. If the teacher has analyzed the task skillfully and has made "a good match" between the reading task and the child's capacity, the child will get satisfaction from his success; he will not need extrinsic reinforcement or rewards; he will be eager for the next reading experience.

Application

The global approach, when applied to a school or school system, will bring together aims, processes, and teaching methods which are usually studied separately. For example, to improve pupils' proficiency in reading and related language arts, an assistant superintendent of a school district appointed a committee to work on this problem during the summer. After clarifying concepts of language arts, child development in relation to reading, and principles of learning, the committee collected facts about pupil characteristics, background, achievement, and reading autobiographies from a large sample of pupils.

Then the committee went to work in subgroups to 1) state specific, definite listening, speaking, writing, and reading behavior appropriate to the abilities and needs of pupils in their classes; 2) analyze the learning process by which each of these objectives could be acquired; and 3) describe teaching procedures that would help pupils to acquire the needed competencies.

Take for example the listening objective "to recognize the *tw* sound in words". The committee analyzed the process into these steps:

1. recognize the *tw* sound in a key word,
2. identify the *tw* sound in other words,
3. distinguish the *tw* sound from other initial sounds in words, and
4. apply this knowledge to the pronunciation of new words in sentences.

The teaching procedure stems directly from this analysis of the behavioral objectives.

Other behavioral objectives on a more advanced reading level are analyzed and taught with similar concern for the child's learning process. Take, for example, the objective: "ability to locate and interpret clues of character in literature." An analysis of the task would include the following:

1. knowing common clues to character and motive, such as appearance, voice, speech, actions, and responses of others to him;
2. having the ability to locate and interpret these clues; and
3. having the vocabulary to express the characteristics.

The teaching procedure may begin with the concrete portrayal of a character in a film or on television. Then the teacher and pupils together read a story, locate verbal clues — at first simple and obvious ones — and discuss their interpretation. They write in columns all the words that the author uses in speaking of each of the characters. They dramatize some of these words to make them more vivid and memorable. By repeatedly going through this process with increasingly difficult materials, the pupils gain proficiency which they can apply in their independent reading.

Individuals need different proportions of programed instruction and steps of different sizes. Able learners can be exposed to the full complexity of language; they can discover relationships and create their own structure of the selection as a whole. Less able learners need to begin at a more concrete level and proceed step by step. All need to take initiative and responsibility for their own learning and not feel that the tasks have been imposed upon them from the outside.

The teaching of reading is not a subject for debate but for research and thoughtful discussion. We are not concerned with whether one method is better than another but with how association of the spoken language with its written symbols is correlated with meaning from the beginning of the learning-teaching process. We should take a global, not a separatist, approach; we should recognize the contribution of sociology, linguistics, teachers' experiences, and children's introspective-retrospective verbalization, as well as the contribution of psychology to the improvement of reading. Then we shall have a surer basis for 1) stating definitely what children should learn; 2) analyzing their learning tasks, and 3) discovering ways to assist children in their own learning. Our analyses should be continually modified and extended by the children's responses to our teaching and their analyses of their successful learning.

When a teacher asked one little boy about his reading, he said, "If I could read better, I'd 'preciate myself more". By bridging the existing gap between psychological theory and practice we may prevent much failure and discouragement on the part of children.

REFERENCES

1. Clymer, Theodore. "What Is 'Reading'? Some Current Concepts", in Helen M. Robinson (Ed.), *Innovation and Change In Reading Instruction*. The Sixty-seventh Yearbook of the National Society for the Study of Education, Part 2. Chicago: University of Chicago Press, 1968.
2. Hegge, T. G.; S. A. Kirk; and W. D. Kirk. *Remedial Reading Drills*. Ann Arbor, Michigan: George Wahr, 1940.
3. Inhelder, Barbel, and Jean Piaget. *The Growth of Logical Thinking from Childhood to Adolescence*. New York: Basic Books, 1958.
4. Kirk, S. A., and J. J. McCarthy. *Illinois Test of Psycholinguistic Abilities* (revised). Urban, Illinois: Institute for Research on Exceptional Children, University of Illinois, 1968.
5. McCullough, Constance M. "Balanced Reading Development" in Helen M. Robinson (Ed.), *Innovation and Change in Reading Instruction*. The Sixty-seventh Yearbook of the National Society for the Study of Education, Part 2. Chicago: University of Chicago Press, 1968.
6. MacKinnon, A. R. *How Do Children Learn to Read? An Experimental Investigation of Children's Early Growth in Awareness of the Meanings of Printed Symbols*. Toronto, Canada: M. Cupp Clark, 1959.
7. Richards, I. S. "The Secret of 'Feed Forward' ", *Saturday Review*, February 3, 1968, 14—17.

BEGINNING READING

Joyce M. Morris

33 DEENA CLOSE, QUEEN'S DRIVE
LONDON, W.3,
ENGLAND

Beginning Reading in England

IN ENGLAND, THE RELATED QUESTIONS of when and how to begin teaching children to read have been controversial issues for a long time. But, never before have they been debated so widely and with such vigour as in the period since the First World Congress on Reading because, during this period, the reports of several major inquiries with implications for beginning reading were published and, understandably, received and continue to receive a great amount of publicity. The purpose of this paper is not only to outline the situation but to critically appraise it.

The official view

Six months after the Paris congress, the Central Advisory Council for Education reported its findings on the whole subject of primary education in England (1). These findings are based on the analysis of a vast amount of data collected, at the request of the government, from numerous authoritative sources of research and opinion and in various ways, including observations in schools. Accordingly, what the Plowden Report has to say about beginning reading in English state schools may be regarded as the "official view" and, as such, is a very influential one meriting prime consideration in any discussion of this topic.

A Language Arts Approach. The Plowden Report advocates a language arts approach to reading, one in which reading is not considered in isolation from listening, speaking, and writing. Hence, it approves the practice in many infant schools (for children age five to seven inclusive) of introducing pupils to the techniques of reading and writing *simultaneously,* but only *after* they have achieved a reasonable command of the spoken language.

The Concept of Readiness. Clearly, the Plowden Report supports the concept of "readiness" which, especially when defined in terms of mental age, has been strongly challenged in England during the past five years. However, although the report states that reading and writing skills "can best be taught when the need for them is evident to children", it corrects the mistaken view that *all* teachers have to do is wait until their pupils virtually *ask* for instruction. Teachers are reminded that they must provide a rich classroom environment for the development of language skills and *actively* lead children to acquire these skills.

As to the assessment of reading readiness, no suggestion is given that tests should be administered. This thinking is not surprising since the official view on the use of tests, in general, is that "the business of the school is not to test but to teach". This belief is also in accord with the opinion of most infant teachers that formal tests of any kind are out of place in their classrooms.

Methods. With regard to the instruction which follows an *informal* introduction to reading, the Plowden Report advises teachers to try *all* the methods available to them and not to depend on any one method. The report also, suggests that the criteria for the selection of methods should be the age, interest, and ability of individual pupils.

No mention is made of the fact that the nature of the English language, particularly the irregularities of the grapheme-phoneme relation, must also be taken into account when teaching children to read. This omission may be due to the official view that education should be "child-centred" rather than "subject-orientated". Nevertheless, the report implies support for the majority of teachers who favour methods which emphasise getting meaning from print from the beginning as opposed to those which stress learning the printed code for the spoken language.

Basal Schemes. Most infant teachers use basal reading schemes. The Plowden Report stresses that these should never determine the practices adopted for all children. There should be a range of published schemes with different characteristics in each classroom so that the teacher can choose carefully to suit individual needs.

About the primers and supplementary material available for beginning readers, the Plowden Report is very critical. "Too often the difficult problem of combining interest with a controlled vocabulary is not solved. The middle-class world represented by the text and illustrations is often alien to the children, the characters shadowy, the content babyish, the text pedestrian and lacking in rhythm; and there is rarely the action or the humour which can carry children to the end of the books." Accordingly, research is recommended into the types of primer which are most effective with children from different backgrounds and with varying levels of ability.

Programmed Texts and Machines. Programmed texts and machines for beginning readers are recent innovations in England and, as yet, are used mainly by children taking part in experiments. However, even if research proves their effectiveness, and their relatively high cost is reduced to compete with basal schemes, it is unlikely that these tests will achieve widespread popularity at least for some time. The reason is that to many infant teachers, programmed learning presented in books or by machines seems to run counter to the current trend toward basing children's learning on interest and discovery. Moreover, the Plowden Report, while pointing out the advantage of these innovations in that they can be used individually, suggests that, pending research evidence, these tests probably are more appropriate for developing the reading ability of older backward pupils.

The Initial Teaching Alphabet. No experiments in almost a century of compulsory education in England have attracted more public attention and caused greater controversy than those which began eight years ago with the initial teaching alphabet. It was hoped, therefore, that the Plowden Report would offer guidance on the use of i. t. a., which is designed to make the initial stages of learning to read easier by regularising and simplifying the written code for English phonemes. Why then does it not do so? The reason given is that it would be inopportune to make an assessment since the Schools Council has undertaken an investigation of *all* the evidence available on i. t .a. and the results are not yet available.

There is wisdom in this cautious attitude, but a sentence which follows the brief statement on i. t. a. suggests that proof of the medium's value in promoting a quicker start with reading would not necessarily meet with official approval. The sentence reads: "It is important to stress that even if methods are found which make possible an early beginning in reading, it does not follow that children's time is best spent on reading."

Opposition

Two reports, in a sense, represent "opposition" to the official view of beginning reading.

The i. t. a. Symposium. Soon after the Plowden Report appeared, the first definitive report on London University's five-year experiment with the initial teaching alphabet was published (2). This report is appropriately called *The i. t. a. Symposium,* since it includes critical evaluations of the results by eleven impartial educational experts from Britain, the United States, and the Commonwealth.

Downing, who directed the experiment, states that the following generalized conclusions seem to be supported reasonably well by the results.

1. As an example of a transitional writing system for beginning reading and writing in English i. t. a. generally produces superior results in t. o. (traditional orthography) reading and in t. o. spelling by the end of the third year in school. (At this stage of schooling children have usually reached their eighth birthday.)
2. The success of i. t. a. in improving t. o. literacy skills occurs in spite of an important setback in the growth of these basic skills at the stage of transition from i. t. a. to t. o.

3. The traditional orthography of English is a serious cause of difficulty in the early stages of learning to read and write.

In a summary of the evaluations, Wall points out that the majority of contributors agree that defects in the design of the investigation are not so serious as to invalidate the results completely. He also suggests that these defects may have "reduced the clearcutness of the conclusions and limited rather than undermined their validity". Thus, on the whole, the verdict on i. t. a. from this experiment appears to be favourable, and the medium is now used in an estimated 12 percent of English schools.

Colour Story Reading. Last year, too, a research report was published (3) which suggests that a better system than i. t. a. has been developed for overcoming the special problems of English orthography in beginning reading because it achieves at least equally satisfactory results without changing the alphabet. This system is called *Colour Story Reading* to draw attention to the fact that it uses phonetic colour and is prefaced by nineteen stories which, when read or related to children, provide them with concrete images for the sounds. Major experimentation with this system began in 1959 under the auspices of London University and government sponsorship.

Are changes necessary?

Naturally, debate about the reports on *Colour Story Reading* and i. t. a. has reminded teachers that in 1962 England produced another simplified and regularized system, namely, *Words in Colour* (4). This system has also revived interest in the earlier "phonic-word method" which exploits the regularity that exists in English through phonicallygraded material (5). However, a research report entitled *Reading in Infant Classes* (6), also published in 1967, indicates that the majority of teachers are so strongly committed to the principles and practices outlined in the Plowden Report that extensive, radical changes are not likely in the near future.

Today's burning question, therefore, is, "Are such changes necessary?" In other words, "Should *all* infant teachers, instead of the present minority, use methods, materials, and media which, from the beginning, stress learning a printed code for the spoken language?" The investigations mentioned suggest an affirmative answer if the prime objective of infant schooling is to give children an early start with reading. The same answer is also supported by Jeanne Chall's critical review of research from the laboratory, classroom, and clinic, recently published in her book, *Learning to Read: The Great Debate* (7).

But, should an early start with reading be the prime objective of infant schooling? For different reasons, the Plowden Report implies "No" while the report to be discussed next implies "Yes".

Prognosis for Late Beginners. In December 1966, the National Foundation for Educational Research published *Standards and Progress in Reading,* the final report on a ten-year programme of extensive and intensive studies in the reading field (8). This publication indicates a very poor prognosis for children who have not mastered the basic mechanics of reading by the age of eight, after three years of schooling. At best, the chances of their eventually achieving average or normal competence are about one in eight, and at least half will remain retarded readers to the end of their school days.

Thus, the foundation's report underlines the importance of the early acquisition of reading ability. It also reveals the reasons why the future dismal prospects of about ten percent of the child population appears to be determined at the age of eight. These reasons may be summarised as follows: Late beginners in reading with the greatest number of personal handicaps not only come from the least propitious homes but also have the most unsatisfactory schooling in terms of the reading materials, classroom conditions, and teachers provided for them.

Educational provision for children who have experienced failure in learning to read can and must be improved in ways suggested by the findings of this research. Even then, since "prevention is better than cure", changes in majority practice to give children an early start with reading would seem to be necessary.

Proposed changes

However, since the Plowden Report implies that changes are not necessary, it is important to point out that the report makes recommendations for changes in other aspects of children's schooling which would particularly help slow starters in reading. For example, it recommends that schools in the poorer neighbourhoods, where the majority of these children are to be found, should be given a more generous allowance for reading materials, improvements to school buildings, and the like. The report also recognises that these schools need a greater share of the nation's teaching talent and so, in the hope of attracting teachers of high calibre to work in them, proposes extra remuneration for those who do so.

Besides advocating a national policy of positive discrimination in favour of schools for the underprivileged, the Plowden Report recommends a reorganisation of all primary schools into "first" and "middle" schools, catering for pupils aged five to nine and nine to thirteen, respectively. Beginning readers would therefore have an extra year of "infant" education in which to reach the stage of being able to make progress on their own. Under the present system, recent research shows that about half the seven-year-olds transferred from infant to junior classes have not progressed beyond primer three of a basal reading scheme (9).

The extension of part-time nursery education for the under-fives is another important recommendation. This extension would give thousands of children who fall into the category of the "culturally-deprived" opportunities to develop a command of the spoken language before entering "first" schools where reading and writing are introduced. These children would also benefit especially from other proposed changes, such as, a reduction in the average size of primary classes from forty to thirty.

Unfortunately, the Plowden path to progress is paved with excellent recommendations which, with few exceptions, would cost many more millions of pounds to translate into actuality than the government can afford to allocate from the national budget in the present economic situation. Therefore only the first few steps along this path have been taken so far.

In the circumstances, it is fortunate that there is one road to progress which would not cost any extra money to follow. This road is to give top priority to the teaching of reading when preservice and inservice courses for teachers are planned. Only when *all* teachers in infant or "first" schools have the necessary "specialist" knowledge and expertise to carry out their most important task can one rest assured that *all* children have a better-than-even chance of a good send-off on the road to becoming effective readers. When this day dawns, the great debate in England about the "when" and "how" of teaching beginners to read will have lost some of its fire and may even be resolved.

REFERENCES

1. Department of Education and Science. *Children and Their Primary Schools.* A Report of the Central Advisory Council for Education. London: H. M. Stationery Office, 1967.
2. Downing, J. *The i.t.a. Symposium.* Research Report on the British Experiment with i.t.a. Slough: National Foundation for Educational Research in England and Wales, 1967.
3. Jones, J. K. *Research Report on Colour Story Reading.* London: Nelson, 1967.
4. Gattegno, C. *Words in Colour.* Reading: Educational Explorers, 1962.
5. Daniels, J. C., and H. Diack. *The Royal Road Readers.* London: Chatto and Windus, 1954.
6. Goodacre, E. J. *Reading in Infant Classes.* A Survey of the Teaching Practice and Conditions in 100 Schools and Departments. Slough: National Foundation for Educational Research in England and Wales, 1967.
7. Chall, Jeanne, *Learning to Read:* The Great Debate. New York: McGraw Hill, 1967.
8. Morris, Joyce M. *Standards and Progress in Reading.* Studies of Children's Reading Standards and Progress in Relation to their Individual Attributes, Home Circumstances, and School Conditions. Slough: National Foundation for Educational Research in England and Wales, 1966.
9. Kellmer Pringle, M. L., et al. *11,000 Seven-Year-Olds.* First Report of the National Child Development Study (1958 Cohort). London: Longmans, 1966.

May F. Marshall

Claremont Teachers College
Perth, Western Australia

Countdown to Reading

THE PARALLEL BETWEEN PREPARATION for reading and preparation for launching a space capsule is not as fanciful as it may seem. Both require highly skilled, dedicated, and intelligent personnel; both involve vitally important timing; and both require a knowledge of causes of error and how to remedy them.

This report concerns the reading readiness program being carried out in Western Australia, whose centralized system of education is often criticised by overseas educators until they realize that, with the vast distances and scattered population, this system happens to be, for the present, the only way to ensure that all children in the states have an equal educational opportunity.

Children are admitted to school in the year in which they turn six and, in general, are admitted in February. This population poses many problems for the first grade teacher because of its chronological age range of one year and much wider range mentally. In some cases where large numbers of children are admitted, children are grouped in three groups according to age. The main point to note, however, is that in Western Australia one has always taught the five-year-old to read even while teachers elsewhere were emphasizing that a mental age of about six years and six months, even seven years, was optimum for initial success in reading. This emphasis on mental age led to the belief that "time was in charge of readiness"; consequently, teachers frequently delayed teaching reading until the moment of readiness had passed.

It appears that children who are ready for an early start in reading do not seem to suffer from an adverse effect when taught; on the contrary, they appear to profit from activities which stimulate their interests in reading. Durrell has suggested that the widespread misinformation about "wait until the child is ready" probably is the greatest single cause of reading disability.

Goals

Before considering a program of preparation, it might be well to consider the goals. Intelligent planning is required to reach the designed target economically and efficiently; and in considering any reading program, one must pause to ask why one teaches reading.

29

The day is past when one can be satisfied with teaching the basic skills. With ever-increasing speed it is becoming more and more vital to the individual to be able to read and to read well. Two interrelated types of aims were given educators by Gray, aims concerned with values to be secured through reading and aims concerned with the development of reading attitudes and skills needed to attain these values.

The early period is so vital in establishing values and skills in those children who, for various reasons, find it difficult to learn that one cannot help but be concerned when one realizes the tremendous power for effective or non-effective teaching which rests with the first grade teacher. The need for highly skilled teachers is essential, and research has found that teacher competence, among other things, is highly related to reading achievement. It is the teacher who is responsible for the effectiveness of the program, who makes effective or indifferent use of the materials, who can surpass the progress and needs of her pupils — in short, it is the teacher who can inspire them to want to read and who should be able to conduct them through the stages to the final "countdown". This type of teacher presupposes teacher training and practical experience and constant refreshment through inservice education.

Other factors which play a part in this stage of reading are a desire to read, visual and auditory discrimination, a background of experience, language, social and emotional experience, freedom from physical defects, a sense of accomplishment, interesting materials which provide for a systematic sequential development of reading skills, and consideration of the size of the class and the classroom organization.

While the list of factors has not been exhausted and while there are differences of opinion on the value of various aspects, there seems to be unanimity on the importance of having adequate preparation before a child is placed on the "launching pad" of beginning reading. Possibly the most important factor is that which recognizes the combined need for developing the whole child and the responsibility of the teacher to provide suitable activities and stimulating but careful guidance.

With these factors in mind, the writer will trace the program entitled *Readiness for Formal Work* being carried out in Western Australia and, by means of this practical approach, deal with the factors involved. It must be emphasized at the outset that the writer is not speaking for all of Australia, for each Australian state has its own system of education; but time did not permit the writer's visiting all the states or writing to them and collating the information.

The material set down in the booklet provided for the guidance of teachers represents an attempt to develop a readiness program for first grade. This booklet is suggestive rather than prescriptive. At no time is it intended that teachers should follow the booklet rigidly. The program, which covers a period of twelve weeks and for purposes of organization is divided into six units, provides for the progressive development of the various skills and experiences. Teachers are urged to introduce through the various suggested practices the main characters and essential nouns of the introductory book of the basic series. In a research school where i. t. a. has been used with success for some years, the suggestions made can be adapted to the situation.

Regular revision and checking are recommended, and teachers are urged to enrich suggested activities. It is hoped that by giving such guidance to young teachers and to teachers who return after many years away from the profession, children can be helped to reach the point of maturity at which "formal" school work will be both pleasurable and successful. For children who can read or who have reached the level of maturity necessary to read, the program need only be used as a framework for the teacher to provide a great variety of experiences.

This stage is very important in Western Australia because of the age of admission and the fact that approximately less than twenty percent of four- and five-year-olds receive any kindergarten experience.

Aims of Program

The general aims include the social adjustment of the child and his preparation for learning formal subjects through auditory and visual discrimination, language, manipulatory skills, social studies, music, physical education, and mathematics. The medium used is a nursery rhyme and its associated activities. Nursery rhymes are known to most children and provide a happy core of activities. These rhymes can be recited, sung, danced to; the people and objects mentioned lend themselves to illustration, modeling, drawing, counting, and manipulation; and the reading materials, to exercises in word and phrase recognition. Even on the first day at school a child's eagerness "to read" is satisfied because with help he can "read" a rhyme.

Children are introduced to listening exercises, including instruction, listening to stories, letter stories, musical instruments, initial sounds, rhyming words, building of alphabet books — all as a preparation for the teaching of phonics. Although these rhymes and their associated activities have now been combined in a booklet, other books are also suggested to ensure that the work does not become too prescribed. A wide range of reading materials, such as large picture books, pictures with simple captions, story books, teachers' books, and experience booklets, are recommended so that children can gain a feeling of context or sequence — all to encourage a rich language experience which necessarily precedes reading. In this age children of five and six are exposed to so much experience, not dreamed of in a former day, that they have a richer background. Therefore, these booklets are essential. One of their values — and there are many others — is that every child who comes to school brings his own unique experiences which affect his ability to learn to read, and gradually he learns what print is for. These booklets provide, also, a guide to the teacher's understanding of the experiences and influences to which her children have been subjected, as shown, for example, by the sentence of a five-year-old, "We went down to the Fremantle wharf to see the Star Billabong being loaded with pig iron by big magnets". The language-experience approach is invaluable when one is teaching native and migrant children.

The specific aims are concerned with the growth of knowledge and the development of attitudes and interests, habits and skills; and as many of these aims are obtained only by observation, teachers are urged to observe the children and to record progress, as such information is invaluable in evaluating the success of the course.

Children are helped to become independent, to develop a sense of responsibility, to speak clearly, to recognize their own names and belongings, to respond to direction, to work and play within a group, to use classroom equipment, to match and recognize words and phrases, and to discriminate between words such as "high", "low", "quick", "slow', and the initial and final sound in any given word.

Great importance is attached to the teachers role. Actually, this role cannot be overestimated in giving the child security and ensuring that the classroom is bright and attractive rather than a passive, static environment which does little to stimulate a child to reach out for experiences which help him to expand and grow. Too many teachers underestimate the drive to learn within children. Much help with equipment and its uses is given to teachers. Much of the equipment is simple and easily acquired and, therefore, manageable in all schools. Generally, it is accepted that this preparatory work helps to eliminate much of the confusion that used to exist.

We have found that "setting out" the skills in a horizontal position in the booklet ensures that all receive due emphasis. Visual discrimination, and frequently auditory discrimination, has always had appeal. Yet, although both are so necessary to phonics teaching, they have been neglected or treated cursorily. One of the criteria for a successful program is the evaluation of the child's progress. One measure used is a short group test for readiness given by the teacher, with parts of it being given individually. The results of readiness tests cannot be used alone to group children for reading instruction. Performance on certain aspects of the tests which seem to be related to reading growth, such as letter and word matching, appear to make the greatest contribution to predicting reading success.

Concluding Statement

This description shows one attempt to ensure that children are being helped to read better. It is not the only way but it does try to cater to individual differences. A. Sterl Artley has said "There would be logic in the extension of the readiness concept downward for some in the same way that we extend it upwards for others". Helen Murphy has suggested "Readiness is not something we wait for, but rather something we must bring about through careful instruction", and Durrell has indicated that "Reading readiness is not a mysterious glow that descends upon a child; it is a series of specific perceptual abilities which can be given by direct teaching".

There are, however, several pressing needs before all children can reach the target of being able to read. One is the need to make provision for children who, because of an arbitrary age of admission to school, are being deprived of the opportunity to learn and yet may be ready to begin reading. Another is the need for teachers to be more adequately prepared to teach children to read, particularly those teachers responsible for this very important and challenging stage of beginning reading. This is a matter for concern, so much so that the writer urges you to join Mary Austin's "Torch Lighters" and not rest until more time is devoted to the professional education of teachers of reading. Other needs are for a greater understanding of child development and its relation to the reading program, greater creativity on the part of teachers, and a greater application of research. When these prerequisites have been met, most children will be launched happily and successfully into reading — a human right.

RUTH TREVOR

DEPARTMENT OF EDUCATION
WELLINGTON, NEW ZEALAND

An Eclectic Approach to Beginning Reading

IT IS GENERALLY ACCEPTED that research raises more questions than it answers. Nevertheless, one is inclined to expect too much from research and too little from the proper exercise of the wit of man. The findings of research into the learning and teaching of reading must be interpreted and applied in conjunction with what is already known about children's development, theories of teaching and learning, the nature of reading and language, and individual differences among both those who learn and those who teach.

Readers will be familiar with the conclusions that have been drawn from the studies of a number of approaches to beginning reading instruction carried out in the United States during the past three years. Those conclusions that seem of particular importance at this time include the following:

1. that significant numbers of children learned to read by each of the approaches studied;
2. that no particular approach stood out as being superior to others;
3. that no approach resulted in all children successfully learning;
4. that no approach succeeded in providing for all reading requirements; and
5. that of greater importance than the particular approach was the quality of the teaching.

Training Teachers

Obviously, therefore, one must concentrate resources on training teachers of reading and on providing continuous inservice support and advice. Also, instead of expending attention, energy, and finance on a search for *the best method,* one should select and use the best of what is available.

One of the marks of a professional person is that he regards his clients as individuals and seeks to understand and prescribe for the needs of each. This attitude is conceivably much easier for the architect, the lawyer, and the doctor to maintain than it is for the teacher. Nevertheless, one must consider the

34

ways of providing for the educational needs of each child. Educators have known about individual differences a long time and the earlier attempts to meet these differences through the familiar Dalton and Winnetka Plans. But more recent insight into the intellectual and emotional development of children and of the ways in which they learn, emphasises the need to do much more than rearrange the subject matter. Ways of relating reading materials, child development theories, and grouping devices so that teachers may individualise their teaching are needed. This approach seems a more practical solution to the problem of catering to individual differences rather than attempting complete individualisation of the reading programme.

As differences exist among children, so do differences exist among teachers. Some teachers are knowledgeable and well able to choose methods and materials and make arrangements to ensure that children will embark successfully upon the reading task. These teachers are aware of the reactions of each child to the teaching programme and are able to judge the time professional help and advice should be sought. Other teachers, needing much more guidance and support, are less knowledgeable, less sensitive to children's reactions, and less able to understand and provide for the needs of the children. Those responsible for the training and supervision of teachers must be just as sensitive to individual differences among teachers and just as well able to provide for these differences as teachers are expected to be where the children are concerned.

Teaching Methods

Chall's book *Learning to Read: The Great Debate* is heralded as "the most important book on American education for the past ten years". Although parts of the book are absorbing, particularly the section on basal readers and the chapter describing the author's observation of the teaching of reading in British and American classrooms, the writer disagrees with Chall's conclusions and recommendations. Her interpretation of research as supporting a code-based emphasis in beginning reading instruction will, alas, strengthen the hands of those with plans to produce yet more methods and materials to aid word mastery.

Anyone learning to read can hardly avoid the code. But can educators not take the view that a child new to reading should use what he has already discovered about language — the meaning of what he hears, his interest in sounds and words, his facility with talking, as well as his newly learned audiovisual skills to help him master the code? And is not the purpose of breaking the code to get the message?

Since the early 1950's, most of the innovations in reading instruction have had to do with the business of word mastery and are largely attempts in one form or another to make the code consistent and regular through the use of

colour, additional symbols, new letter-forms, or markings of some kind. Sometimes the words are arranged and introduced according to particular linguistic patterns as in the "can, Nan, fan, Dan" materials.

These attempts to simplify language and learning, based primarily on association theories of learning, may well make more difficult the task of understanding the relationship between written and spoken language and deriving
meaning from reading. Children learning from such materials may be robbed
of opportunities to generalise and to discover for themselves the soundsymbol
associations.

It would seem reasonable, therefore, that any approach to beginning reading should take account of such current learning theories as those of Piaget
and the developmental psychologists and should be concerned *both* with
making sense and getting the intended meaning *and,* inescapably, with learning letter-sound relationships. The importance of reading, it has been stated,
lies not in the fact that reading is the manifestation of mechanical skills but
rather that it affords an efficient medium for thinking and learning.

When reading is seen as a process closely akin to thinking, as an aspect of
language, and except for the printed symbol similar to listening, it seems sensible both to introduce children to reading and to continue the teaching and
learning of reading through methods and materials which challenge and develop interests and intellectual powers, make use of and add to experiences, and
depend upon and increase understanding and use of spoken language.

The Eclectic Approach

After some years of experience in working with children who have failed
in reading and, later, with classroom teachers of reading at all levels in both
elementary and secondary schools, as well as from observations of the teaching
of reading in overseas countries and from the study of the professional literature, the writer has come to the conclusion that there is no single approach,
set of materials, or arrangement of children that will meet all or even most
of these requirements. So it would seem the present task is one of selecting
elements from various approaches and synthesising these into a reading programme. Such an eclectic approach to the teaching of reading at all levels
makes possible a variation in methods and materials as well as in timing, pacing, and organisation and caters to the differences in readiness for reading,
in learning rate, in language development, in interests, and in attitudes
among children. It enables one, therefore, to select approaches, techniques,
and materials that work well; that accord with the principles of child development, the reading process, and the structure of the language; and that meet
the needs of the children.

What then are the components of such an eclectic approach to the teaching
and learning of reading? By beginning with the children's language and their

experiences, by stimulating talking and discussion, and by writing what children say about the things they do and are interested in, the teacher introduces them to printed symbols. Soon they understand what reading is and what significance it has for them. There are elements here from the language-experience approach. By frequent rereading of these written records they learn to recognise printed words, both those with particular significance for them and those that are less interesting, the high-frequency service words. Some of the children are soon ready to read books, at first picture-and-caption books and then simple storybooks and the best of the basal readers. Provision is thus made for different stages of readiness and rates of learning, for varying interests, and for the teaching and practice of the skills that are needed to understand what is read, to identify new words, and to consolidate old ones; children are helped to discover letter-sound associations and to use these, especially as beginning sounds, together with the meaning to work out the words that are new in printed form only and for which they already have meanings. Reading is introduced as an aspect of language and is closely related to the experiences and the interests of the children. The pace is suited to the children's abilities and needs, and use is made of a varity of materials and teaching techniques. From the outset there is thinking while reading, personal involvement in the stories and other content, a mixture of conversation and reading, and systematic introduction and development of skills. With such a well-structured programme neither teachers nor children need depend entirely upon a basal reader but may draw from other sources for what is needed for a variety of reasons at different times. Children are involved in early writing that has a personal flavour; many opportunities are presented for developing good listening and good talking. A language arts approach is used which represents an attempt to make learning to read an exciting adventure for children. What description of this method could be better than Carl Aage Larsen's? When talking about beginning reading in Denmark, he said, "In the first steps towards literacy it is important to foster the attitude in the child that reading is basically a sublime form of guessing as it is even at the advanced level ... a meaningful text is indispensable and cannot be replaced by nonsense syllables or inane sentences ..."

How is one to decide the relative merits of the various methods, materials, and grouping devices that are available? Above all, this process of selection must not be hurried. It must involve children who will be using them and teachers whose knowledge of the teaching of reading, of the professional literature, and of the findings of research may be wider than is possible for most classroom practitioners. One must not be taken in by the somewhat extravagant claims sometimes made by the authors and promoters of these things but must examine both the claims and the goods to see how far they agree. And answers must be found to such questions as these: 1) Does anything have to be unlearned? 2) What evidence do the promoters offer to support their claims? 3) What is the validity of such evidence? 4) What is the history of this particular approach or set of materials? Gates has suggested that most of them have long lines of ancestry.

A method or a set of materials or, indeed, a grouping device should neither be accepted because it is new nor rejected because it is old. Most of the time both the old and the new have some value, for some teachers and some children.

READING COMPREHENSION

Marion D. Jenkinson

University of Alberta
Edmonton, Alberta
Canada

Basic Elements of Reading Comprehension

The enormity of the presumption of attempting to condense into such a short paper the research and knowledge concerning some of the elements of reading comprehension is overwhelming. Although I have attempted to do what a French critic described as "the art of not saying everything", I can only hope that I shall not distort through distillation either fact or theory.

It is a paradox, however, that, as noted in the recent National Society for the Study of Education yearbook (26), though there is a plethora of research into beginning reading and particularly word recognition, there is still a paucity of research into the area of reading comprehension. One of the reasons for this lack lies in the nature of the complexity of this activity, for its performance is usually less overt and leaves much to be examined indirectly by inference. Moreover, until comparatively recently there has been the frequent assumption that if words are decoded, meaning will be automatically understood. Furthermore, this area of study is plagued by the problems attendant on research in the frontier of any field (14).

It is proposed to examine briefly three elements basic to the understanding of reading comprehension: the nature of comprehension and the factors involved, the measurement of reading comprehension, and the bedrock of comprehension-word knowledge.

The Nature of Comprehension and the Factors Involved

Currently there has been a recurrence of debate concerning the nature and definition of the act of reading. From the days of Thorndike (40) it has generally been accepted on the North American continent that reading is a type of thinking which is triggered by printed symbols which represent words. The nature of the thinking aroused by reading is still a major point of debate. Yet thinking in reading is a specific, controlled activity, the control being dependent upon the thoughts engendered by the material read.

Many experts have given summaries of the cognitive processes believed to

41

be involved in the reading process. One of the best known is that by Gates (9):

> ...However, to say that reading is a thought getting process is to give it too restricted a description. It should be developed as a complex organization of patterns of higher mental processes. It can and should embrace all types of thinking, evaluating, imagining, reasoning, and problem solving. Indeed it is believed that reading is one of the best media for cultivating many techniques of thinking and evaluating.

Some researchers, following the early view of Thorndike (3), tend to concentrate on reading as a type of problem solving. They suggest that the reader defines the problems when he assesses the author's purpose for writing, determines his own purpose in reading, and proceeds through the traditional problem-solving steps. Other writers have been reading in terms of a confluence of convergent and divergent thinking (11, 32). The convergent occurs because the reader must lay his mind open to the precise meaning that the author is presenting, but the reader's thinking may become divergent when he reacts to and then assimilates the ideas from the material.

There have also been attempts to transpose general classifications of thinking directly to reading. Thus it has been suggested that associative thinking, convergent thinking, divergent thinking, problem solving, and creative thinking all take place at some time in the reading act (27, 37).

Yet another way of examining reading is to look at it in terms of a systems approach and to see reading as featuring both an open and closed system (15). This attitude requires extrapolation, interpolation, and reinterpretation in the light of the reader's reaction.

Considerable stress has been placed by others on the cognitive problems involved in both inferring and deriving meaning through both interpretation and extrapolation. Barrett has presented a taxonomy of reading comprehension which details eight types of inference (5). This taxonomy also emphasizes the problems of reasoning in reading and suggests that the reader must be aware of the logical and psychological problems involved in the ideas presented.

Though most of the research has tended to stress the cognitive aspect of the process, some attention has been directed to the affective domain which must be part of appreciation. Studies which have revealed this matter have usually been concerned with the factors that are involved in reading literature (10, 34, 35, 41).

The diversity and lack of consensus concerning underlying theory make a synthesis of the findings difficult. However, an attempt will be made to summarize these factors under four headings: general factors, language factors, factors inherent in the material, and factors within the reader.

The General Factors in Reading Comprehension. One of the earliest distinctions made as a result of research findings was that critical reading abilities were distinct from general reading abilities (*4, 6*). Factor analysis of comprehension tests have an almost unanimous finding of a factor which is labelled "abstract reasoning" (*6*). Fairly early, too, it was established that though there was a minimal general factor in reading comprehension, major differences arose with respect to reading in various content fields. This finding has more recently been reinforced by Davis' recent research (*7*). It is obvious that, as far as cognitive processes are concerned, each substantive field of knowledge will present different modes of thinking when presented in written form.

One other factor appears to be that the cognitive nature of the writer's thought does not necessarily elicit an identical mode of thought response in the reader. However, this assumption has rarely been investigated in depth, although several pieces of research, mostly still unpublished in the form of doctoral dissertations, indicate it is probably so. A major factor in comprehension errors committed by readers may be their failure to be able to identify or empathize with the thought of the writer. A further problem occurs, too, in that there may be cognitive limitations of the reader in terms either of his developmental maturity or of his unfamiliarity with the topic of the material (*16, 21, 24, 38*).

Language Factors in Comprehension. One of the major problems in assessing reading comprehension is to differentiate between the factors which are involved in language acquisition and those which are closely connected with the difficulties encountered in reading comprehension. As yet, research has revealed few of the differences between the spoken and written language. Linguists have frequently commented upon this variation, but only recently have some of them begun to indicate, in sufficient detail, the nature of the differences between spoken and written language. Abercrombie's comments (*1*) are particularly pertinent to some of the aspects of written language which may inhibit comprehension. There still remains a yet larger problem — that of the nature of verbal understanding as a whole. This area has received scant attention possibly, as Russell suggests (*28*), because the complexity of the field is so great that few have attempted to understand what is still intrinsically a mystery of how thought is conveyed by words from one human being to another.

The recent work of several psychologists in the area of language and cognition may begin to yield much pertinent information for future researchers in reading. Several factor-analysis studies have isolated "word" factors concerned primarily with knowledge of vocabulary (*3, 18*) and, in addition, a "verbal" factor which appears to contribute to the ability to see interrelationships among ideas represented by words in context but which does not involve much abstract reasoning.

The Problems Inherent in the Material. The genre or type of presentation which the author chooses to use, in addition to the constraints of the cognitive discipline under which he is operating, may present many problems to readers who are unaware of the nature and impact of these controlling factors (*13*). Not only the substantive content, however, but also the level and concentration of concept presentation may form a barrier (*23*). In addition, the tone of the writer and his attitude towards both his subject and towards the reader, all apparently affect the level of comprehension (*20, 39*). Again, though several studies have suggested this phenomenon, few have examined the question in sufficient detail. Consequently, only generalizations, so vague that they are almost impossible to translate into direct practice, can be made.

Factors Within the Reader. Though studies here are more numerous, they are not very extensive. The results suggest that not only intelligence but appropriate levels of cognitive development, including vocabulary and concept formation, are prerequisites to comprehension (*12*). Several years ago, Russell (*29*) suggested that "in all probability an inadequate vocabulary is the greatest single cause for failure to read with comprehension in either the general or technical field". Research since has substantiated this comment in detail, but further work has also shown an adequate knowledge of vocabulary depends on the depth and breadth of meaning as well as on the ability to understand the meaning of the word in use or in context (*30*).

Several recent studies have shown that comprehension is subject to the biases and attitudes of the reader and that such prejudices may be a product of the total environment, both within and without the schools which surround the child (*8, 22*). It has also been shown that both the interest and the purposes of the reader will affect the level of his comprehension (*33*). Yet, while single studies have revealed this factor, there is not sufficient weight of evidence, as yet, to indicate the nature of the problem of determining bias, attitudes, interest, purposes, or prejudices and how to influence this. There are still not sufficient cumulative research results upon which one can proceed with sufficient security.

Some recent research with respect to the factors within the individual reader has attempted to examine the impact of the psychological notion of cognitive style and to attempt to assess how this work will reflect the ability of the reader to read critically or independently (*19, 42*).

One of the most productive ways of analyzing problems encountered by readers either within the material or themselves has been to analyze the errors that readers make. It has been in this area, perhaps more than in any other, that ingenious attempts have been made, including the retrospective and introspective comments of the readers themselves, on the processes that they appeared to be using as they read (16, 24).

Strang (36: 69) has summarized the insights which have been gained from this research, and which differentiate the able from less able reader. However, the research into reading comprehension has been for the most part on the product rather than the processes involved. In the past decade more attention has been paid to processes. Yet whatever the focus of the research, the results cannot be independent of the measures used to assess comprehension.

The Measurement of Reading Comprehension

One of the major techniques used in studying comprehension has been through the means of tests, and, consequently, much of the research in reading has been concerned with the construction and evaluation of reading tests.

A frequent complaint voiced by current researchers is that most of the traditional standardized tests do not measure the type of cognitive thinking process that is involved in such activities as critical reading (17). As a result most investigators devise their own measuring instruments. Though these have usually been very carefully constructed and have been checked for reliability, the nature of the validity of these tests is not always clear-cut. Since construct validity requires an accumulation of information and this is obviously lacking, the problems then become compounded.

Most researchers develop their objectives or hypotheses and then construct tests which will measure these specifically. However, few researchers have attempted to use tests devised by someone else, for such tests, the researchers argue, are not appropriate to their particular research. The time has come when it is essential that some more general measures which have greater percogent thrusts forward result rather than spasmodic individual forays in isotinence to the cognitive processes in reading must be developed. A further problem arises in assessing the validity of the tests because of the problem of the nature of and type of transfer from general cognitive processes to those which may be involved in reading.

An even more difficult problem with respect to measurement may arise from the nature or type of response by which one measures achievement. For the most part, the response mode is that of asking questions, but such a method presumes that the respondent understands the question accurately. It has also been well documented that these interrogative techniques may, in fact, structure the respondent's thinking and thus his reaction to what he reads. There have been some attempts to use such things as the cloze procedure (25, 31) or to ask general questions which are open-ended and do not require a single correct answer. It would seem, however, that there is a great need for ingenuity in devising not only more appropriate tests but more appropriate response modes for measuring all the varied facets of reading comprehension.

Conclusion

Brevity may be the "soul of wit", but it is not conducive to thorough treatment of this vast topic. Current knowledge of this important area is like a fifteenth century map of the world — a mixture of truth and error. In future research one must map the terrain and chart the seas carefully so that cohesive, cogent thrusts forward result rather than spasmodic individual forays in isolated areas. To paraphrase Tennyson, it seems to the writer that this research " . . . is an arch where through gleams that untravelled world whose margin fades for ever and for ever when I move".

REFERENCES

1. Abercrombie, D. *Studies in Phonetics and Linguistics.* Oxford University Press, 1965.
2. Ames, W. "The Development of a Classification Scheme of Contextual Aids", *Reading Research Quarterly*, 11 (Fall 1966), 57—82.
3. Anderson, C. C. "A Factorial Analysis of Reading", *British Journal of Educational Psychology*, 19 (1949), 220—221.
4. Artley, A. S. "A Study of Certain Relationships Between General Reading Comprehension and Reading Comprehension in Specific Subject Matter Areas", unplublished doctoral dissertation, State College, Pennsylvania, 1942.
5. Barrett, T. C. "Taxonomy of Cognitive and Affective Dimensions of Reading Comprehension", quoted by T. C. Clymer in "What is Reading? Some Current Concepts", in *Innovation and Change in Reading Instruction*. N.S.S.E. Yearbook, op. cit.
6. Davis, F. B. "Fundamental Factors of Comprehension in Reading", *Psychometrika*, 9 (September 1944), 187—197.
7. Davis, F. B. *Identification and Measurement of Reading Skills of High School Students.* Cooperative Research Project No. 3023. Philadelphia: University of Pennsylvania, 1967.
8. Gans, R. *A Study of Critical Reading Comprehension in the Intermediate Grades.* New York: Bureau of Publications, Teachers' College, Columbia University, 1952.
9. Gates, A. I. "Character and Purposes of the Yearbook", *Reading in the Elementary School*. N.S.S.E. 48th Yearbook, Part 2. Chicago: University of Chicago Press, 1949.
10. Gray, W. S., and B. Rogers. *Maturity in Reading*. Chicago: University of Chicago Press, 1956.
11. Guilford, J. P. "Frontiers in Thinking that Teachers Should Know About", *Reading Teacher*, 13 (February 1960), 176—182.
12. Hall, W. E., and F. P. Robinson. "An Analytical Approach to the Study of Reading Skills", Journal of Educational Psychology, 36 (1943), 429—442.
13. Harris, C. D. "Measurement of Comprehension of Literature: Studies of Measurement of Comprehension", *School Review*, 56 (May and June 1948), 280—289, 332—342.
14. Jenkinson, Marion D. "Reading: An Eternal Dynamic", paper presented at the presentation of the N.S.S.E. Yearbook, Boston, April 1968.
15. Jenkinson, Marion D. "Reading: Developing the Mind", in J. Allen Figurel (Ed.), *Changing Concepts in Reading Instruction*. Proceedings of the International Reading Association, 1961. (New York Scholastic Magazines.)
16. Jenkinson, Marion D. "Selected Processes and Difficulties of Reading Comprehension", unpublished doctoral dissertation, University of Chicago, 1957.

17. King, M. L., B. D. Ellinger, and W. Wolf. *Critical Reading*. Philadelphia: Lippincott, 1967.
18. Langsam, R. S. "A Factorial Analysis of Reading Ability", unpublished doctoral dissertation, New York University, 1941.
19. Lundsteen, S. W., and W. B. Mitchell. "Validation of Three Tests of Cognitive Style in Verbalization for Third and Sixth Grades", *Educational and Psychological Measurement*, 26, No. 2, 1966.
20. McCaul, Robert L. "Effect of Attitudes Upon Reading Interpretation", *Journal of Educational Research*, 37 (February 1944).
21. McCullough, Constance. "Responses of Elementary School Children to Common Types of Reading Comprehension Questions," *Journal of Educational Research*, 51 (September 1957), 65—70.
22. McKillop, A. S. The Relationship Between the Readers' Attitudes and Certain Types of Reading Response", New York: Bureau of Publications, Teachers College, Columbia University, 1952.
23. Maney, E. "Literal and Critical Reading in Science", *Journal of Experimental Education*, 27 (1958), 57—64.
24. Piekarz, J. A. "Getting Meaning from Reading", *Elementary School Journal*, 56 (March 1956), 303—309.
25. Rankin, E. F. "The Cloze Procedure — A Survey of Research", in E. L. Thurston and L. E. Hafner (Eds.), *The Philosophical and Sociological Bases of Reading*, 14th Yearbook of the National Reading Conference, Milwaukee, 1965.
26. Robinson, Helen M. *Innovation and Change in Reading Instruction*, N.S.S.E. 67th Yearbook, Part 2. Chicago: University of Chicago Press, 1968.
27. Russell, David H. "Higher Mental Processes", in C. W. Harris (Ed.), *Encyclopedia of Educational Research*. New York: Macmillan, 1960, 654—661.
28. Russell, D. H. "Resarch of the Process of Thinking with Some Applications to Reading", *Elementary English*, 42 (April 1965), 370—378, 432.
29. Russell, D. H., and H. R. Fea. "Research on Teaching Reading", in N. L. Gage (Ed.), *Handbook of Research on Teaching*. Chicago: Rand McNally, 1963.
30. Russell, D. H. *The Dimensions of Children's Meaning Vocabularis in Grades Four Through Twelve*, University of California Series in Education No. 5. Berkeley: University of California Press, 1954.
31. Schneyer, J. W. "Use of Cloze Procedure for Improving Reading Comprehension", *Reading Teacher*, 19 (December 1965), 174—179.
32. Smith, D. E. quoted in G. D. Spache. *Toward Better Reading*. Champaign, Illinois: Garrard Publishing, 1963, 67.
33. Smith, H. K. *Instruction of High School Subjects in Reading for Different Purposes*, The University of Chicago Cooperative Research Project 1714, U.S. Office of Education, 1967.
34. Squire, J. R. *The Responses of Adolescents While Reading Four Short Stories*, Research Project No. 2. Champaign, Illinois: National Council of Teachers of English, 1964.
35. Strang, Ruth. *Exploration of Reading Patterns*. Chicago: University of Chicago Press, 1942.
36. Strang, Ruth. "The Reading Process and Its Ramifications", in *Invitational Adresses 1965*, Newark, Delaware: International Reading Association.
37. Stauffer, Russell G. "Critical Reading at Upper Levels", *The Instructor*, 74 (March 1965), 74—75, 101.
38. Swain, E. "Conscious Thought Processes Used in the Interpretation of Reading Materials", unpublished doctoral dissertation, University of Chicago, 1953.
39. Thayer, L. O., and N. H. Pronko. "Factors Affecting Conceptual Perception in Reading", *Journal of General Psychology*, 61 (July 1959), 51—59.
40. Thorndike, E. L. "Reading as Reasoning: A Study of Mistakes in Paragraph Reading", *Journal of Educational Psychology* (June 1917), 323—332.
41. Wilson, J. R. "Responses of College Freshmen to Three Novels", unpublished doctoral dissertation, University of California, Berkeley, 1962.
42. Wolf, W., C. Huck, and M. L. King. *Critical Reading*. Philadelphia: Lippincott, 1967.

CHARLOTTE S. HUCK

THE OHIO STATE UNIVERSITY
COLUMBUS, OHIO
UNITED STATES OF AMERICA

Teaching Critical Thinking Through Reading

A GROUP OF SEVEN-YEAR-OLDS read three different accounts of the story of Betsy Ross and the making of the first American flag. One book stated that George Washington showed the design to Betsy Ross and asked her to make the new flag; a second book began with the statement that some historians believe Betsy Ross made the first Stars and Stripes but that no one is sure if she really did while a third book maintained that it took Betsy Ross just one day to make the first American flag. After comparing these three books, one child remarked, "Well, they can't all be right; that's for sure". Asked which book they would recommend, the children agreed that the one that indicates that historians are not really certain who did make the first American flag would probably be the most reliable source.

These children were engaged in the process of critical thinking. They were comparing three accounts of a subject, noting differences and similarities,, drawing conclusions, and making a judgment concerning the validity of the presentations. The stimulus for the critical thinking and the data for making their decision came from conflicting statements that these children had *read*. By skillful questioning and by the use of appropriate materials, an intelligent teacher had lead children to evaluate their reading and make a judgment about it. These three components are necessary to train students in the skills of critical reading: namely, 1) children who know how to establish criteria for evaluating what they read, 2) materials that lend themselves to this kind of treatment, and 3) teachers who know and understand the strategies for teaching critical reading.

The Process of Critical Thinking

Not all thinking is critical in nature. In Guilford's classic (9) article on "The Three Faces of the Intellect", he describes 120 independent kinds of thinking of which critical thinking is included among the evaluative abilities. These evaluative abilities are described as the ability to make judgments concerning the accuracy, goodness, or workability of information. In the book *Taxonomy of Educational Objectives,* Bloom and his associates (4) attempted to classify all types of thinking under the six categories of knowledge, comprehension, application, analysis, synthesis, and evaluation. They saw these categories as sequential and cumulative, with the evaluation category at the top of the scale but including all the lower kinds of thought processes. Russell (16) specifically defined critical thinking as a three-factor ability which includes an attitude factor of questioning and suspended judgment, a conative or functional factor which involves use of methods of logical inquiry and problem solving, and a judgment factor of evaluating in terms of some norm or standard or concensus.

A Definition of Critical Reading

Critical reading has been described as critical thinking applied to the act of reading. Smith (17) placed critical reading at the highest level in a hierarchy of reading comprehension skills, including: 1) literal reading (understanding the denotation of words, ideas, or sentences in context); 2) interpretative reading (obtaining deeper meanings not directly stated in the text); and 3) critical reading (evaluating the quality, the value, the accuracy, and the truthfulness of what is read). The most concise definition of critical reading has been given by Helen Robinson (15). She states that "Critical reading is the judgment of the veracity, validity, or worth of what is read, based on sound criteria or standards developed through previous experiences". The working definition that developed from a three-year study of *The Critical Reading Ability of Elementary School Children* (24) at Ohio State University states that

> Critical reading is an analytical, evaluation type of reading in which the reader analyzes and judges both the content of what is stated and the effectiveness of the manner in which the material is presented. Reading critically involves searching for the purposes underlying the author's message and making rational judgments about what is read based upon valid criteria. Critical reading skills can be applied to argumentative, informational, or literary materials.

Teaching Critical Reading

Critical thinking skills do not merely develop with maturity; they must be carefully nurtured, planned, and taught. Some persons associate critical thinking with particular subjects — the inquiry method of science or social studies, for example. Yet critical thinking is too important to total lives to be somehow relegated to one period or one subject a day. How foolish it would be to develop critical scientists who were noncritical readers! Educators need to plan a curriculum in which children are given frequent opportunities for critical thinking. Since the majority of teachers spend one fourth to one sixth of their time teaching reading, it would seem most important to teach critical thinking skills through reading. Hopefully, too, the student will continue the habit of critical reading throughout his adult life, whereas he may discontinue the study of science, mathematics, or social studies with the completion of his school courses.

In the past, a great deal of time has been spent in developing the mechanical skills of reading and very little time in developing thoughtful, discriminating, critical readers. Schools have produced generations of children who never go beyond the literal interpretation of "what the book says". Education has failed to teach the child that reading is much more than the sum of its facts. Getting the facts is not critical reading, but determining whether one is reading facts, opinions, or assumptions is setting the stage for critical reading. Sensing the relationship among the facts, determining which are relevant to his particular needs, comparing the facts to his background of experience and knowledge, and finally weighing these facts against others and arriving at a conclusion — these are all skills that go far beyond the literal reading of a text, important skills that need to be taught.

Knowledge of Forms of Writing

One of the first steps required of a critical reader is to determine the literary form of what he is reading. Is he reading prose or poetry, fiction or nonfiction, an editorial or a news report, a fantasy or a realistic story, a biography or an autobiography? He needs to discover that the author's purpose for writing will differ with various types of writing and that different criteria for evaluation apply to different genre. For example, in evaluating a fairy tale, one would not look for character development or gradual change in characterization, for characters in fairy tales are usually stereotypes, symbolic of good and evil: *all* princesses are beautiful; *all* stepmothers, evil; and *all* fairy godmothers, kind and loving. Yet a criterion by which one would evaluate such realistic fiction as Ester Weir's *The Loner* (22) is the believability of the character change of David. The reader would first have to know the form of writing before he could evaluate the quality of writing.

A group of third graders (eight-year-olds) were given an assignment to write an article on any season of the year. One child began his paper with the rather uninspired statement that "Spring was the most beautiful time of the year", and he read no further when his classmates took him to task for not recognizing the requirements of the assignment. He had been asked to write an article, not give a biased opinion. He could say that some persons believe spring is the most beautiful time of the year or that he thought it was, but he could not factually state such a thought in an article. His classmates pointed out that some areas of the world did not even have spring or that other persons might think another season was more beautiful. The discussion that followed the reading of this particular exercise was filled with fine critical thinking based upon these children's knowledge of the criteria for a particular form of writing.

Knowledge of the Quality of Writing

After recognizing the form of the writing, children then have to be helped to establish criteria for what constitutes fine writing. The components of good writing of fiction usually include 1) a well-constructed plot, 2) convincing characterization, 3) significant theme, and 4) appropriate style.

Children most frequently read a book for its plot or story, but how many of them know what constitutes a well-constructed plot? Even young children can identify the differences in such accumulative plots as "The House That Jack Built" or the repetitive action of such folktales as "The Three Goats Gruff" or "The Three Little Pigs" in which everything happens in triplicate. Older students may compare a straight-forward plot with one that utilizes a flashback sequence. One group of ten-year-olds charted the many parallel plots in the exciting Australian story of an uncontrolled fire in the book *Ash Road* (*18*) by Ivan Southall.

Children can learn to distinguish between excellent character *delineation,* such as seen in *Madeline* (*2*) by Bemelmans or *Pippi Longstocking* (*11*) by Astrid Lindgren; the superb character *development,* as exemplified by the story of Chibi in *Crow Boy* (*25*) by Yashima; or the painful maturing of Stephen de Beauville in Barbara Picard's haunting story *One Is One* (*13*).

The theme of a story is frequently difficult for young children to generalize. Only when six-year-olds *compared* books that had a similar theme, such as *Dandelion* (*6*) with *Harry The Dirty Dog* (*26*) or the *Rabbit That Wanted Red Wings* (*1*), did they realize that very different stories could still have the same theme. All these tales are the stories of dissatisfied animals who try to be something other than themselves; only when they are true to their own natures, do they find happiness. One first grader, when asked how these stories were alike, replied: "Well, all the main characters tried to wear disguises!"

Just as children learn to identify and evaluate the use of persuasive words in advertisements and editorials, they need to learn to evaluate the use of such literary devices as point of view, metaphor, and symbolism. Younger children may try telling well-known stories from different points of view; for example, the story of "The Three Bears" as Goldilocks might tell her mother or as the Little Bear might tell it in sharing period the next day at school! Nine- and ten-year-olds can evaluate the shift of point of view in the poem "Abraham Lincoln" by the Bénets (*3*). In the first verse, Lincoln is discussed by his contemporaries who did not recognize greatness when it lived among them: "Need a man for troubled times/Well, I guess we do./Wonder who we'll ever find/Yes, I wonder who". The last verse is written from the point of view of the poet today who comments: "That is how they met and talked/ Knowing and unknowing/Lincoln was the green pine/Lincoln kept on growing".

Knowledge of the writing requirement of nonfiction is necessary for evaluation also. Children may be helped to discover that textbooks, news items, encyclopedias, and almanacs present facts but seldom reveal the feelings surrounding these facts. The purpose of such books is to inform. Editorials, advertisements, and cartoons present opinion, and their purpose is to persuade or convince. The children easily learn the seven basic propaganda techniques including the use of 1) "bad names", 2) "glad names", 3) "transfer", 4) "the testimonial", 5) "plain folks", 6) "card stacking", and 7) the "band wagon". They may apply this knowledge as they write advertisements or editorials of their own. Clarity of writing and organization of informational materials should be evaluated. Pictures and charts should be analyzed and judged for their details and presentation of data. Why were these pictures included? What do they show? What impression did the photographer wish to make? What have you learned from this picture? These are some of the questions children should be asking about the many pictorial presentations which are increasingly a part of reading matter.

Knowledge of the Content

One cannot evaluate the form without the substance nor the container without the contents. Critical readers will establish criteria for judging both what is said and how it is said. Frequently, the criteria for evaluating the content of literature must come from the life experiences of the child or other books. He may compare the story of *The Bully on Barkham Street* (9) by Mary Stolz to his own encounter with a bully — is that the way bullies usually act? Is that the way others act toward them? Or the reader may compare the escapades of those all-American boys Henry Reed (*14*) and Homer Price (*12*) with Tom Sawyer (*21*) — how are they alike? How are they different? Have you ever had any experiences similar to theirs? One needs to help children build a literary framework against which they can measure other books. How is *Charlotte's Web* (*23*) by E. B. White like *Wind in the Willows* (*8*)? Both *Early Thunder* (*7*) by Jean Fritz and *Johnny Tremain* (*5*) by Esther Forbes are about the American Revolutionary War, but in what ways are they different? How are the events in this story like those in your history books? How are they different? Gradually children begin to see that the content of literature is more than just exciting stories; it is the ageless chronicle of man's living and striving.

Both nonfiction and fiction must be judged for accuracy of facts. The teacher who wants to develop the skills of critical reading searches for such conflicting statements as found in the Betsy Ross stories. She helps children compare the facts presented in one account with those presented in another. One group of nine-year-olds listed the facts presented in editorials and advertisements and, then, in a second column, the facts that were omitted. Reading a bicycle ad they noticed that the bike cost $39.95 and could be purchased for $1.50 a week, but the notice neglected to tell how many weeks the buyer would have to pay. When checking informational books on dinosaurs, these children found which books clearly distinguished fact from theories about the disappearance of the dinosaur and which ones mixed the two. Stereotyped presentations may still be discovered in many social studies books. Phrases such as "all Scottish people are thrifty", or "the Arab nomads exist by robbing others", or "American Indians always walk in single file" suggest an all-or-none way of unscientific thinking. The critical reader will learn to look for such questionable generalizations.

In reading nonfiction, particularly, the background of the author needs to be known. Children need to ask if this particular person is qualified to write on new developments in space rockets. In one classroom, children entered into a spirited discussion on who would be the best qualified person to frite a book for children about France — a native of France, a visitor to France, an American who had lived in Paris for a year, a professional writer, or a professional writer who had visited France. The list became more and more demanding, and these children were quite critical of backgrounds of the authors of books which they had obtained from the library. Most important, they learned that a person's writing grows out of his background and experience and usually represents a particular point of view.

Strategies for Teaching Critical Reading

Children do not obtain this background of knowledge unless they are taught, nor do they utilize this knowledge to develop sound criteria for evaluating their reading unless they are encouraged to do so. And they do not learn to apply these criteria to their reading except as a teacher values and teaches critical reading.

Teachers themselves must know the process of critical reading, have a thorough knowledge of appropriate materials, and understand the stragegy for teaching this kind of behavior. The seven-year-olds who were comparing the biographies of Betsy Ross did not just happen to find them. The teacher knew of these conflicting statements and by skillful questioning helped students determine differences in books and come to some conclusion concerning them.

Teachers need to acquaint themselves with the types of questions that are the most thought provoking and the most helpful in causing a child to reflect more deeply. Hilda Taba (20) and her associates in their study of children's thinking concluded that the nature of the questions teachers asked " ... has a singular impact on the progression of thought in the classroom". There is a place for literal questions provided the answers to these questions will lead children to higher levels of thinking. The Ohio State University study of the *Critical Reading Ability of Elementary School Children* revealed that the kinds of questions teachers asked were significantly related to the level of thinking that the children generated. Teachers who asked only for the repetition of material read received short memory-type responses, while teachers who asked children to analyze, compare, and contrast or to synthesize, generalize, and draw conclusions elicited higher-level responses. In this study, teachers learned to ask better questions, and children responded with more evaluative-type answers. The *process* of identifying the facts, interpreting and inferring, analyzing and generalizing, and evaluating and criticizing appeared to be more important than any one type of question, however.

Conclusions

Since the undisputed function of education in a democratic society is to teach persons to think, it seems equally necessary to teach them to think about what they read. In this paper, critical reading has been difined as the analysis and evaluation of both the content and structure of fiction and nonfiction materials. It is a process involving both knowledge of criteria for evaluation and skill in applying them. The thoughtful reader is not just the result of maturation; he is the product of planned instruction. Materials must be carefully selected, and teaching strategies that will raise the level of children's thinking must be developed. Teachers can improve the quality of their questioning and so improve the quality of children's reading. Generally, schools have assumed the responsibility for teaching children *how* to read; now educators must be willing to take the time to teach children to be discriminating, critical readers. For only then will the act of reading be complete.

REFERENCES

1. Bailey, Carolyn Sherwin. *The Little Rabbit Who Wanted Red Wings.* New York: Platt and Munk, 1945.
2. Bemelmans, Ludwig. *Madeline.* New York: Viking Press, 1939.
3. Benet, Rosemary, and Stephen Vincent. *A Book of Americans.* New York: Holt, Rinehart and Winston, 1933.
4. Bloom, Benjamin, et. al. *Taxonomy of Educational Objectives Handbook I: Cognitive Domain.* New York: David McKay, 1956.
5. Forbes, Esther. *Johnny Tremain.* Boston: Houghton Mifflin, 1946.
6. Freeman, Don. *Dandelion.* New York: Viking, 1964.
7. Fritz, Jean. *Early Thunder.* New York: Coward McCann, 1967.

8. Grahame, Kenneth. *The Wind in the Willows.* New York: Scribner's 1908.
9. Guilford, J. P. "Three Faces of the Intellect", *American Psychologist,* 14 (1959), 469—479.
10. Konigburg, E. L., *Jennifer, Hecate, Macbeth, William McKinley and Me, Elizabeth.* New York: Atheneum, 1967.
11. Lindgren, Astrid. *Pippi Longstocking.* New York: Viking Press, 1950.
12. McCloskey, Robert. *Homer Price.* New York: Viking, 1943.
13. Picard, Barbara. *One Is One.* New York: Holt, Rinehart and Winston, 1966.
14. Robertson, Keith. *Henry Reed, Inc.* New York: Viking, 1958.
15. Robinson, Helen M. "Developing Critical Readers", in Russell G. Stauffer (Comp.), *Dimensions of Critical Reading.* Proceedings of the Annual Education and Reading Conferences, 11 (1964), 1—12. Newark, Delaware: University of Delaware.
16. Russell, David H. "The Prerequisite: Knowing How to Read Critically", *Elementary English,* 40 (1963), 579—597.
17. Smith, Nila Banton. "What is Critical Reading?" *Elementary English,* 40 (April 1963), 409—410.
18. Southall, Ivan. *Ash Road.* New York: St. Martin's, 1966.
19. Stolz, Mary S. *The Bully on Barkham Street.* New York: Harper and Row, 1960.
20. Taba, Hilda, et al. *Thinking in the Elementary School.* San Francisco State College, Cooperative Research Project 1574. Washington, D.C.: Office of Education, 177.
21. Twain, Mark. *The Adventures of Tom Sawyer.* New York: Harper and Row, 1876.
22. Weir, Ester. *The Loner.* New York: David McKay, 1963.
23. White, E. B. *Charlotte's Web.* New York: Harper, 1952.
24. Wolf, Willavene, Charlotte S. Huck, and Martha L. King. *Critical Reading Ability Elementary School Children.* The Ohio State University Cooperative Research Project 2612. Washington, D.C.: Office of Education, 1967.
25. Yashima, Taro. *Crow Boy.* New York: Viking Press, 1955.
26. Zion, Gene. *Harry the Dirty Dog.* New York: Harper and Row, 1956.

Dorothy M. Dietrich

UNION FREE SCHOOL DISTRICT
UNIONDALE, NEW YORK
UNITED STATES OF AMERICA

Developing Reading Comprehension, Ages 8–14

It is usually assumed that by eight years of age most children have acquired the basic decoding skills which permit fuller attention to be devoted to comprehension. Also, by this time a child's thinking and reasoning ability have developed to the stage at which he is more able to cope with deeper and more complex aspects of understanding. Since the major goal of the reading program is the development of reading comprehension and the development of lifetime reading habits, it is important that much time and attention be devoted to this skill.

There are many definitions and models proposed which interpret and define comprehension. One of the earliest definitions, still widely used, is that by Thorndike who said that "reading is thinking". Some have defined levels of comprehension as including literal, interpretive, and critical aspects. Kerfoot (3) in a careful examination of the literature deduced that there are many definitions given for comprehension and many ways of classifying comprehension skills. Since there seemed to be great differences in both the theoretical base as well as the descriptive terms used, he states it is often difficult to establish a sound basic philosophy of comprehension unless one stays with a particular authority.

Cleland (1) proposed a model to explain the intellectual processes used by the reader to gain meaning. His six points included 1) perception — the meaningful response to the graphic symbol; 2) apperception — relating new material to one's previous background of experience; 3) abstraction — the selection or rejection of perceptions, impressions, or concepts; 4) appraisal — synthesizing and evaluating the new materials; 5) ideation — using the ideas in several modes of thinking; and 6) application — the functional use of the ideas gained.

Using Cleland's model, it is then possible to construct an ouutline of procedures to be used by the teacher in developing comprehension skills. It must be remembered, though, that comprehension does not develop unless guidance is provided with all types of reading materials in a most consistent fashion.

Introduction of unfamiliar word forms and unfamiliar concepts. Words with irregular spelling patterns which cannot be easily decoded by the pupils will need to be introduced. Meanings of these words as well as new meanings for words with familiar forms should be discussed.

Review and discussion of pupil's experiential background on the topic. Prior to the reading of any selection the pupils should review the knowledge and concepts that can be used to bring further meaning to the task. With younger pupils it is often necessary to spend considerably more time at this step than with older pupils. There is often need for such questions as, "Remember what we were reading yesterday? (last week? last month?)".

Presentation of purposes for reading. At this time the teacher presents to the pupils the purposes for which the selection is to be read. The purposes or questions posed should be clearly stated and require the pupils to read for broad purposes rather than narrow ones.

Discussion. Following the silent reading of the selection, the teacher's role becomes most important. At this time he must question in such a manner that all aspects of the material are discussed, new ideas and associations made, new concepts developed, problems solved, deductions made, facts evaluated, and judgments and generalizations made.

Application. This often forgotten step is the most crucial one. If children cannot utilize or apply the information gleaned, then the reading has had little value. Teachers must be certain that pupils apply the new knowledge in functional ways that also permit appraisal of how effectively the skills of comprehension are being taught.

Techniques for Teaching Reading Comprehension

In developing a sound reading program the teacher then becomes the medium by which a good theoretical curriculum is put into practice. The many variables involved in developing comprehension demand that discussion is necessary if the teacher is to evaluate the type of thinking in which the child is engaging. This activity militates against the constant use of workbooks and worksheets which demand short answers. The major difficulty is that many teachers themselves have not read widely enough to understand fully the role of comprehension and its various aspects and thus are unable to help children develop the type of thinking skills needed for adequate reading.

In a study done by Guszak (2) on teacher questioning and reading, he found that teachers expend much time and energy questioning literal comprehension dealing mostly with trivial facts. He also noted that students become extremely sensitive in determining what the teacher is seeking and found that students provided answers they thought the teacher expected. He also noted that teachers appear to be conditioning students to take a position without weighing all evidence and without being able to support the position assumed.

In teaching comprehension skills to children ages eight through fourteen, it is important 1) that the teacher be aware of the skills needed to be developed, 2) that numerous ways of developing comprehension skills be used, and 3) that there be careful planning as well as adequate familiarity with the material. Children must understand the various levels of comprehension — literal, interpretive, and critical. By skillful questioning, the teacher should lead children to the awareness of the literal understanding of the material through the use of such words as *who, what, where,* and *when.* The next step is to help children make interpretations based upon their literal understandings. They must be able to see cause and effect relationships, make inference, anticipate outcomes, make judgments, draw conclusions, recognize the author's purpose, recognize the mood of the selection, react emotionally, and the like. When children are able to interpret the material read and to express their thoughts clearly and succinctly, they should then be led to the third level of comprehension where they are asked to react critically by evaluating or making judgments based upon the selection read. This last level of comprehension, critical reading, appears to be a very difficult area for many teachers. If one expects children to evaluate, react, and judge, they must be free to express and substantiate their own opinions and ideas. Discussions which allow for freedom of thinking and expression of ideas can be a very threatening situation to teachers who themselves cannot react in this fashion. Teachers sorely need to learn how to become critical readers themselves so that they fully understand the material to be taught.

It is the questioning done by the teacher which is the most important key to developing preliminary and post understanding. The questions posed prior to the actual reading of the material should help the student set his goals. These questions should tell him the level at which reading and thinking should take place, the types of responses expected, and the rate at which the material should be read as well as help him recall previous learnings in the area. After the material has been read, the teacher needs to use a variety of questions which tape the student's understanding of the material. The questions should include those that involve all levels of thinking. It must be remembered that questions pertaining to literal understanding are the easiest for the teacher to pose and the easiest for the students to answer. Questions involving interpretive and critical understandings often are more difficult for the teacher to phrase and resuire more time for pupil response.

In supervising teachers the writer has found that the inexperienced or poorly trained teachers most often 1) ask too many trivial questions which explore only the basic facts in the material; 2) provide the student with no time to think through his answer when interpretive understandings are asked for, accepting instead a very superficial or partial response or, if there is no immediate student response, answering their own question; and 3) pose very few questions which require a critical response to the material read or in which the pupil is asked to substantiate an answer. Frequently the response is poor, begins with "because . . .", or is not probed further by the teacher.

The development of comprehension calls upon the creative and intelligent thinking every teacher should possess. The questioning used by the teacher needs to allow for the type of material being read, the capabilities of the student, and the type of previous training employed. There is a need for quick evaluation on the part of the teacher to decide 1) if the answer is correct; 2) how to help the student amplify the answer if wrong; 3) how the fallacious reasoning took place; and 4) how to help the student reassemble his facts, reevaluate them, and draw new conclusions.

The preceding implies that teachers need a considerable amount of training in what comprehension is, how to question, and how to evaluate wrong answers to provide guidance.

In the United States there has been much material published during the past fifteen years designed to teach and help students practice comprehension skills. Many materials are fine for helping students glean facts, review vocabulary in context, and understand the relationship of ideas; but missing from these programs is the opportunity to develop ideas to their fullest and to react critically to the material presented. Granted, it is often assumed by the authors of such material that the teacher will follow up the seatwork with discussion. This assumption, however, is not often fulfilled, leaving the danger of pupils, developing very stereotyped responses to printed material — responding in a fashion which the students believe the author wants and usually reporting what the author wrote. The development of good comprehension demands an attitude by which divergent thinking is encouraged and expected, opinions and judgments are supported by facts, and interpretations are made on the basis of past experiences.

Another serious problem involves the complete teacher reliance on manuals or guides accompanying basal readers. While such guides are useful to the beginning teacher, the questions suggested for comprehension development are often stereotyped and dull. Since they cannot be written to meet the needs of all pupils, questions are written for the "average". If teachers would learn to use these questions as suggestions of the type to be asked, leading to the development of particular skills, teacher would be more spontaneous and alive.

The means by which one can upgrade the comprehension skills of students depends to a great extent upon the teacher. Students come to school with a greater fund of experiential background than before (in fact, it appears to grow faster than one can utilize it), a greater awareness of the value of books, and a thirst for learning. Teachers must become better informed themselves, better readers, and more skillful professionally to meet the current demand.

REFERENCES

1. Cleland, Donald L. "A Construct of Comprehension", in J. Allen Figurel (Ed.), *Reading and Inquiry,* Proceedings of the International Reading Association, 10 (1965), 59.
2. Guszak, Frank J. "Teacher Questioning and Reading", *Reading Teacher,* 21 (December 1967), 227.
3. Kerfoot, James F. "Problems and Research Considerations in Reading Comprehension", *Reading Teacher,* 18 (January 1965), 250.

ROBERT FARRAR KINDER

STATE DEPARTMENT OF EDUCATION
HARTFORD, CONNECTICUT
UNITED STATES OF AMERICA

Building on Early Reading Skills

ARE THERE ANY READING SKILLS that are exclusively the concern of pupils who are making initial attempts to read? Are there *any* reading skills that have no counterparts for youth at higher levels of education? Probably not. From lists of reading skills and activities for the early and later stages of schooling, similarities seem to emerge.

Oh, yes, there are differences too — but these seem to be differences in the terminology used, the complexity of the task described, the abstraction level of the reading material assigned, and the intelligent skill versatility expected of the reader. The roots of both early and later listings of reading skills seem the same. At early stages of schooling these roots may nourish only a few branches and leaves, but at higher levels they support a thick crown of leafy growth.

Five main roots for ever-growing reading ability are development of skills as they relate to the pupil's purpose for reading, method of attack, comprehension of meaning, evaluation of ideas, and uses of reading. One teaches skills from each of these five areas at the very early stages of schooling; but, in different ways, one also must teach skills from these same areas at higher levels of education. The roots are the same, but at early levels of schooling they support a sapling reader while at later stages of education they support a mature, growing reader.

Purpose for Reading

"Why read this?" is a crucial question for pupils at all stages of education. The beginning reader is helped in identifying one or more reasons for reading a particular selection. These same reasons are still valid at higher levels of education when the more mature reader must be encouraged to identify such reasons for himself. Some of these reasons are to feel more grown-up; to discover what is said; to find out about something (what it is, what to do, what others think); to have fun (with words, incident, character and setting, or ideas); and to stimulate new thoughts and ideas. All meaningful reading is based on the reader's skill in identifying a valid purpose for reading.

61

At higher levels of education, the teacher has responsibility for helping youth take the initiative in setting their own purposes for reading material assigned in class as well as for reading selections of their own choosing. Why read an essay, pages of scientific exposition, or some other particular piece of reading? The manner of reading a selection is based on the reader's understanding of his purpose. If the purpose is not clear, the reading process is in danger of being ineffective. Older, as well as younger, pupils need help in establishing clear and valid purposes for their reading. But the help these pupils need places progressively more and more emphasis on self-reliance in consciously setting these purposes for themselves — a process that readies them for the world beyond school when they must read purposefully on their own.

Method of Attack

At the very early stages of schooling the teacher leads the child very carefully through a reading selection in a systematic way. The teacher makes certain the child has the motivation, experiences, and skills necessary to read successfully each story assigned. The teacher guides him through his reading of that story and supplies appropriate questions and activities that will make the author's words meaningful and memorable. Under teacher guidance the reading selection takes on significance for the child.

At higher levels, a youth must learn to develop and direct his own methods of attack on different types of reading materials read for particular purposes. There are intermediary systems, such as SQ3R and PQRST, in which the child at the middle levels of schooling can be taught a sort of semi-independent attack on certain types of reading material. He learns to follow a preordained system whereby he surveys to get a general impression of the selection he intends to read; formulates questions he hopes to answer by his reading of that selection; reads the selection to get his answers; recites aloud to himself all he can remember from his reading; and, finally, reviews his reading of the selection. Such systems of attack are useful transitions to the development of individual, independent, and effective methods of attack needed by successful adult readers.

Comprehension of Meaning

The skills involved in getting the author's meaning — both literal and implied — are most explicitly detailed for the instruction of those just beginning to learn to read. Most instructional materials for these early stages feature considerable practice in pronouncing and getting accurate meanings of words; figuring the author's meanings for sentences, paragraphs, and longer selections; and making sensible inferences from what the author has said. At this level a great deal of attention is usually given to instruction in phonics, structural analysis, word context, main ideas, and other such skills.

At higher levels of education these very same skills — although, perhaps, slightly altered by more complex and abstract reading selections to which they must be applied — continue to be important. For unfamiliar words he has never seen in print before, the pupil must be taught to examine context, structure, sound, and the dictionary for clues to pronunciation and meaning. He must be taught to look at the arrangement of ideas — chronological, climax, cause-effect, and other ways that ideas are frequently arranged — for clues to a fuller understanding of the author's intent and meaning. The comprehension skills taught at the early stages of education are not, for most pupils, easily and automatically transferred to the more complex, more abstract reading selections that face the reader at higher levels of schooling. Such skills must be taught at higher levels, too!

Evaluation of Ideas

The beginning reader, as well as the reader at the higher level, is concerned with evaluation of selections he reads. At early reading levels, the teacher stimulates the pupil's evaluation of a story by asking questions that encourage him to think about the worth of what the author has written. The beginning reader is asked to answer questions such as these: "Can you tell me about a boy you know who is like the boy in this story?" "Can you tell me why you liked or disliked what happened to the family in this story?" "Who can tell me about something he read on this page that is not correct?" In this way, the teacher of beginning reading directs the children's attention toward evaluation of selections they read.

Evaluation of reading selections also must continue to be an important part of instruction at higher levels of education. The teacher at these levels must encourage youth to question what they read. Pupils on these levels will be using different materials and generally will have a greater background of experience against which they can evaluate passages they read. However, for many older pupils, evaluation of an author's writing is not an automatic process. These pupils do not transfer readily what they have been taught in the early stages of their education to the more difficult selections they read at higher levels. They need instruction that will help them to learn to judge the validity and reliability of adult reading selections. They need to learn to question an author's ideas for their relevance to life and for their significance. Instruction at the higher levels of education should encourage pupils to *gradually* take over more and more responsibility for self-initiative in evaluating ideas.

Uses of Reading

The uses of reading are intimately tied to the reader's purpose in reading. If he has set out to have an enjoyable experience, it is hoped the author has provided something enjoyable. If the reader wanted to learn how to fix a broken spoke in his bicycle wheel, hopefully he found out how. If he intended to discover more than he already knew about words and how they can be put together to give a vivid picture, hopefully the author provided examples which were meaningful. Even for the very young child just beginning to learn to read, reading must have a conscious utility for the reader.

At higher levels of education, the instructional program must feature a variety of uses for reading and, at all times, teachers must help pupils to be aware of why they are reading. Sometimes a selection is read in order to compare an author's ideas with those of the reader or with the ideas of another author. At other times, the reader uses his reading to help him know how to behave at a dance, to understand how wars are started, or to keep himself posted on current events. Reading may have many uses, in addition to just reading for reading's sake.

Summary

Whether it be those concerned with the pupil's purpose for reading, method of attack, comprehension of meaning, evaluation of ideas, or uses for reading, all reading skills have their roots in early schooling. As the child progresses to the higher levels of education, he continues to need instruction in these skills for he must use them in a more sophisticated manner on reading selections that are more varied, more complex, and more abstract. At higher levels of education most readers do not approach their full reading potential unaided. The transition from almost complete dependence on teacher direction for skills development in the early years to independent improvement in these skills must be gradual from year to year until the pupil is ready to take his place in the world of adults. With an effective reading program at higher levels of education which builds on the skills taught in the early years, a youth stands a better chance for making a difference in the adult world — a difference that is better!

THE PREPARATION OF TEACHING MATERIALS

CONSTANCE M. MCCULLOUGH

SAN FRANCISCO STATE COLLEGE
SAN FRANCISCO, CALIFORNIA
UNITED STATES OF AMERICA

The Language of Basal Readers

THIS PAPER will explore some of the thinking one must do in order to decide the language to use in a basal reader and to decide what the child's preparation must be for that language.

A good beginning is to think of the purposes of the basal reader. One purpose certainly is to give experiences that will lead to ease in reading the kinds of material that are available in the literature of that language. The reader series should, as soon as possible, include passages from the great literature in that language — models of many styles, many literary forms, and many moods.

By "as soon as possible" is meant as soon as the wording and meaning in that literature are within the child's grasp. Some people believe that the use of simple words is the only criterion of ease. But words in common use among children may be long and unusual in structure and still be easier than shorter words of less common use. Equally important considerations are the word order within sentences, sentence structures, the interrelationship of ideas, and the level of ideas — concreteness versus abstractness, for example.

The American author, Jessamyn West, has said that good children's literature means something to the adult as well as to the child. One level of meaning, or one facet of meaning, may be within the grasp of the child. The adult should be able to read the same material later with additional pleasure and insight.

If a language group is to have only one basal reader series, that series should probably be in the standard form of the group's language. On this the reader may agree. The point at which one might find marked disagreement about the language of basal readers is at the beginning of the series. How should it start?

There are those who think the readers should start with the natural spoken language of children and only gradually introduce the broader vocabulary of written material. The philosophy underlying this idea is that the use of the natural spoken language in printed form is a natural bridge from hearing language spoken to seeing it written, a bridge that helps the child recognize and understand the printed symbols. For children whose dialect is very much like the standard language, this idea seems ideal. But for children whose dialect is remote from the standard, or even is a foreign language, this practice is less helpful.

Of course, even the dialect speaker may become a more versatile person for the experience, consider the case of a child in a language-impoverished home, that is, a home in which language is rarely used, with the family preferring the silent language of gestures or head movements and whose dialect, when used, is different from standard.

Such a child comes to school and learns to read in the Hindi Reader, "Aap kasa hanh, Pita-ji?" or "How are you, Respected Father?" His own father would not know what was meant, and probably the child would be safer to say it to someone else's father, instead. But this child does learn a respectful form of standard Hindi which will be acceptable in many places.

There is great argument at the present time between those who would start with the standard language and those who would start with a dialect. Those in favor of starting with the dialect say that the child learns more rapidly because he sees his own language in printed form. He accepts more readily the standard language *when he finally learns it.*

Opponents of this view reply that the goal is to teach the reading of the standard language. The dialect may seldom, if ever, be found in books. These people say that the best time to add a language is at about the age of seven. If five to seven years have already passed without formal schooling, why delay longer? Some day television may offer a preschool induction into the standard language; but, meanwhile, a five- to seven-year handicap exists.

Peacemakers have suggested that both approaches can be introduced at once. The child can say something in his own dialect, and the teacher can write what the child has said. Then the teacher can say, "Here is another way of saying it and writing it", and write the same idea in the standard language, saying each word as he writes. Through repetition the child learns to read both versions.

Even this excellent suggestion has its weaknesses. The teacher's ear may not be sufficiently tuned to the child's dialect. The teacher may not hear all the sounds he is to write. The dialect may be one which has never been written. Increasingly, as families move from place to place, teachers meet children of several dialects or even of several foreign languages in one class. It is impossible for the teacher to write in all the other dialects or languages, either in point of time or in point of linguistic knowledge.

Within limits, however, some adjustment is possible. If a teacher has two dialect groups in his class, one of which he knows and one of which he does not know, a good adult speaker of the second dialect may be employed or persuaded to write and interpret what the child wishes to say.

Some educators might say, "Why not use an initial teaching alphabet? Teach the child the symbols for all the sounds in the language, and let him write in that code". This would be a solution for some dialects but not for all. And it would not even offer the symbols for some of the sounds of other languages. If it did, the teacher would have difficulty teaching the symbol for a sound he, himself, could not distinguish.

There are linguists who feel that one should not confine children to one dialect, lest linguistic versatility be crippled. Such linguists encourage teachers to have children learn to speak in more than one way, to be asked a question in a dialect and to answer in the standard language, or vice versa. Teachers attending the meeting of the National Council of Teachers of English in Honolulu last November witnessed a demonstration by third-grade children who were given a sentence in one of several dialects or in standard English — which the teacher termed "Mainstream English" — and they repeated it in pidgin English, Japanese-American, Chinese-American, Italian-American, German-American, or Spanish-American dialect. The quick changes the children were able to make, regardless of their own backgrounds, were impressive.

Is it conceivable that a basal reader series could be written in the standard language in all except the first book and that the first book could be printed in different editions, each for a special dialect. Departure from the dialect might be achieved by a gradual change within the book.

Yes, this plan is conceivable, but there are practical obstacles if the dialect populations are small. Publishing houses are in business. They are not primarily charitable organizations. There is a point beyond which the printing of separate books for a small population becomes charity. There is no profit in it; indeed, there may be a loss. In an ancient country like India and in a relatively new country like the United States of America, to accommodate all language groups and dialect groups without huge government subsidies would be impossible.

It is interesting, however, to consider who benefits and who is discriminated against when one provides a congenial beginning in reading for some children and an uncongenial beginning for many others who either represent numerous small groups or a large minority which has not yet voiced a protest. To the writer's knowledge — which admittedly is limited — there is no reader series in the United States of America designed especially for children of Japanese-American dialect or of Chinese-American dialect. One could continue to name sizable dialect groups which have special needs in beginning the reading of standard English but receive no special help. There are special reader series for the so-called urban child, who lives in the inner city; and the reader has perhaps heard of the special reader series designed in the Detroit city schools for the large Negro population there. But the reason these special readers have been developed is that the groups as social groups were more noticeable. The writer does not believe their needs as dialect groups have yet been met.

Whatever the language of the basal readers, and regardless of the care with which it has been chosen, those who decide upon it have a responsibility to the teacher. That responsibility is to delineate some of the dialect problems and foreign language problems which must be taken care of before the child is expected to read the standard language.

The Reading Project of the National Institute of Education in India surveyed a sampling of children from six Hindi-speaking states to determine the vocabulary and sentence structures in common use. One hundred forty words were found to be common enough to be used in the beginning Hindi Readers. A list was also made of common concepts, such as *mother,* and the forms the teacher might expect to hear in dialects of Hindi.

The Reading Project also developed a reading readiness test, part of which identified the sound distinctions which children have to hear and produce in the Hindi language. Readers of Hindi have to recognize the different printed symbols for two slightly different sounds and realize the different meaning which one sound instead of another evokes when added to the pattern of a word. It was found that most of the Hindi-speaking children in the survey had difficulty distinguishing vowel sounds. Many children had difficulty distinguishing aspirated and unaspirated consonant sounds, such as the *k, g, d,* and *b* (kh, gh, dh, bh). Sounds whose production could readily be observed in the position of the lips seemed to be more clearly distinguishable. This information meant that many Hindi-speaking children needed ear and speech training in their own language before they could be expected to read with accuracy and understanding.

The readiness test in Hindi sounds has special significance in New Delhi, where central government employment draws families from all over India. Thousands of speakers of other regional Indian languages live in that city and send their children to school. The readiness test administered to a large group of children who speak one of these regional languages will show the special problems of sound discrimination which must be met for children of that language group. Teachers of such children can be presented a list of special needs, with suggestions of ways of meeting them. Teachers can also administer the test to individuals or to a whole group and chart the needs.

The reader may think too much is being made of the dialect and language problem in reading. The writer wishes this charge could be true. A few linguists are now turning their attention to the reading problems created by dialect differences. Labov, who studied in detail the Harlem Negro dialect of some boys, found evidence which is indeed startling in its implications for reading.

Imagine yourself as one of these boys looking for the first time at a basal reader. Your initial consonant sounds are standard except for the *th*, pronounced *d*. This substitution of *d* for *th* you share with speakers of a number of other dialects, some of European origin. You and they are fortunate in that you can learn to read *that* as *dat* and *them* as *dem* and *they* as *dey* and still know what is meant.

Your big problem comes at the point beyond the first sound in a word. You pronounce many of your vowels like other vowels, so that words which are different only in the vowel sound are not different as you pronounce them. Both in the middle and at the end of a word, you omit the *r* and *l* sounds: *during* becomes *doing*; *toll* becomes *toe*; *fault* becomes *fought*. *T, d, s* and *z* sounds which account for tense and number signals at the ends of verbs and nouns are not pronounced in that position at all. You give the same treatment to final *g* and final *k*. Final *m* and *n* are nasalized in your dialect — sung through the nose rather than pronounced. Of the 220 words in Dolch's list of basic service words in the English language, your dialect changes 158.

Bad, back, bag, and *bat* are all *ba* to you. If your teacher has Japanese and Chinese speakers in the class, you can join them in work on final consonant sounds and final consonant clusters.

The forms of the verb *to be* baffle you when they appear on the page, for you, as well as Chinese and Spanish speakers, do not use them in speech. You have depended upon words like *yesterday, today,* and *now* to suggest tense and cannot tell from the variant endings or contractions *(he'll)* what time it is. The *apostrophe s* in printed form is news to you, for you have never formed possessives in a special way. You have depended upon number words *(some, ten, many)* to suggest the plural form of a noun *(ten dolla')*.

With all the mysteries that these differences create, you fall behind others in your class and ultimately lose interest in school.

There are some things in your favor. Chances are that you understand your teacher better than he understands you. You are fairly familiar with the intonation of English and the order of an English sentence. Your main problem is that you omit sounds and words, within words and within sentences, that make a great deal of difference to meaning.

Your teacher perhaps finally realizes that you are having difficulty with word endings. He may give you lists of words to read and recite. He corrects your pronunciation. But since the words are listed instead of embedded in a context, you do not know the meaning of the correction and perhaps do not even hear the difference. He may put you into a linguistic reader, with sentences like *that fat rat sat pat.* You say and think *Dat,* and *Dat* was all right for meaning. But words ending all alike just convince you further of the need to look at the front of the word and ignore both the sight and the sound of the ending.

Only a few children who find themselves in such circumstances at the tender age of five or six or seven have the amazingly good fortune and tenacity to overcome the obstacles and to achieve pleasure in literacy and scholarship.

Readiness for the language of the basal reader cannot be the same for all of them. Neither should it be of equal length or timing. The Chinese-speaking child, for example, has more to learn than the Negro dialect speaker. Many of his meaning distinctions are produced tonally rather than by speech sounds. His verb does not change tense at all. Prepositions are news to him. Subordinating conjunctions, such as *when* and *because,* are unknown to his language. This last point alone suggests that his listening and speaking experiences must go beyond basic sentences to complex structures.

Conclusion

In the past, when a child was failing to read, the teacher merely worked harder, but that recipe did not always work. Now educators are beginning to see specific steps to take in diagnosis of learning problems, and some of those steps must be tailored to the difference between the child's dialect and the language of the reader series. It is not enough to do more of what one has always been doing. One must learn to be as directly helpful as the child is needful. Changes in the books themselves cannot be the whole answer, though they are certainly part of it.

When one looks at a great river of fresh water pouring irrevocably into the salt ocean while thousands of acres of land remain desert and when one sees in the colour of the river the precious soil draining from a starving land, the magnitude of the waste appalls. There is another kind of waste, another kind of thirst and starvation in all societies. With intelligence, it can be prevented.

VERA SOUTHGATE BOOTH

UNIVERSITY OF MANCHESTER
MANCHESTER, ENGLAND

Structuring Reading Materials for Beginning Reading

THOSE WHO BELIEVE in the importance of children's learning to read and are concerned with discovering how to best help them master this basic skill undertake the task in many different ways in different countries and, indeed, in a variety of ways in the same country. Yet, all these ways can be divided into two broadly contrasting approaches, identified by an emphasis on either instruction or learning.

Instruction versus Learning

Some approaches give priority to what the teacher should do: which methods should be used; which reading schemes, books, and apparatus should be selected, and how they should be utilised, being considered the most important questions. The teacher is envisaged as the key figure, organising and arranging instruction in beginning reading for pupils. This emphasis springs from the belief that with appropriate instruction children will begin to read. In most countries the majority of teachers align themselves with this belief.

The minority view is to consider first how the child learns rather than how the teacher might teach. It is in line with a Montessori or Froebel approach to learning. The teacher is concerned with providing for children an environment rich in stimulating materials and activities of all kinds, which the children are encouraged to use, manipulate, or explore. A wide variety of books, which the teacher reads to the children and which they freely handle, forms an important part of this environment. It is believed that in this situation children will soon want to learn to read and, with a little encouragement and guidance from the teacher, will succeed in doing so. The process represents a child-centred approach to learning to read, with an emphasis on motivation and individual development. Activity and informality are the keynotes of such classrooms, in marked contrast to the more formal working arrangements usually prevalent when teachers support instruction theories.

The current trend in educational thought in England is away from reading instruction towards a child-centred approach to learning. Such an approach to beginning reading, which is supported by most inspectors and advisers in primary education, is clearly reflected in the recently published Plowden Report (1967) — a full-scale governmental report on primary education in all its aspects. In a volume of some five hundred pages, only five pages deal specifically with reading; and, moreover, only one of these pages relates to "Teaching Children To Read". The learning approach is also exemplified in certain so-called "progressive" infant schools. Even so, the majority of infant classes are rather more formal, and most infant teachers are still concerned with instruction as much as, if not more than, with learning.

There are dangers inherent in both the instruction and the learning approaches. The grave danger, when teachers pin their hopes on instruction, is that they themselves may begin to assume that what has been taught has been learned. One has only to observe either class or group reading instruction taking place to realise the fallacy of this assumption. The proportion of pupil time devoted to features of the environment other than the teacher or the task, and likewise the proportion of the teacher's time devoted to attempts to focus children's attention on her instruction, increases rapidly. With regard to the alternative approach, the prime danger when the emphasis is on learning is the possibility that the teacher will assume that, given a stimulating environment and freedom to explore and experiment, all children will, in time, want to learn to read and be able to do so without specific instruction.

The Need for Structure in Informal Classes

Because of the many advantages for children, the writer strongly supports the growth of these informal, active classes in primary schools. Among the advantages can be listed the importance of individual progress; the highly motivated and purposeful learning carried out with excitement and absorption by children; the development of independence, responsibility, and attitudes of enquiry; the growth in creativity; and the opportunities for social interaction. At the same time, the writer is very conscious of the need for structuring the learning situations within such classes in order to facilitate the process of learning to read. The following points are of relevance in this context.

In the first place, written English does not constitute a regular spelling system. If the written form of this language represented a one-to-one relationship between spoken sound and written symbol, one might have a reasonable basis for hoping that, by heuristic methods, children could be encouraged to discover these relationships and so form generalisations. Such an approach is now being used in the fields of mathematics and science in some primary schools. But in the field of reading, the spelling system actually prevents or discourages children from making generalisations. For example, the child who has just begun to form a mental concept of the letter "a" after meeting it in "cat", "man", and "bag", will quickly have his theory demolished when he comes across words such as "cake", "father", or "water".

Second, even with the use of a regular code or medium for beginning reading, the writer is not convinced that all children will learn to read eventually, and almost incidentally, merely by being placed in the right environment. Brighter and average children may do so, but slower children do need a substantial amount of guidance and some instruction from the teacher, as well as opportunities to work with carefully graded materials planned to give reinforcement and practice, before learning to read.

Third, there is no doubt that the good teacher in the informal infant class does manage to ensure that each child makes progress in reading, according to his individual needs and abilities, in ways which might be described as "incidental learning". Close observations in such a class, however, would show the experienced teacher to be structuring the learning situation for the individual child and particularly for the slower child. It would be seen that both individual diagnosis and planned learning were being carried out intuitively and functionally by this teacher and that, if detailed written records were not being kept, memory was serving the same purpose. Nevertheless, ensuring reading progress for all children, in these conditions, is an extraordinarily difficult task in which younger, less experienced teachers are not always able to succeed. They might work better and their pupils might progress further in a rather more-structured framework. Also, when changes in primary school staffs are frequent, continuity in young children's reading progress is more easily ensured within a planned reading programme, which utilises a certain amount of structured reading materials.

Finally, discovery methods of learning, to be effective, require certain basic skills of which reading is probably the most important, followed closely by knowledge of how to use an index and simple dictionaries and reference books. Young children, even before they have started to read and write, can begin to discover, observe, experiment, and compare; but their progress must necessarily be hampered by lack of these skills. Heuristic methods of learning will be greatly facilitated and can only be fully developed when children are able to read.

Reflections on these points lead the writer to conclude that the freer the atmosphere and working conditions of infant classes, the more important it is that, if young children are to learn to read, three conditions should prevail. First, the teacher should know, in detail, the various stages which the child must master in order to acquire this skill; in other words, she needs a master plan. Second, all the reading materials which form the reading environment should be so structured as to form major or peripheral arts of this plan. Third, the teacher needs to keep meticulous records of individual learning so that each child's progress in the different spheres of reading can be guided and aided. This paper is concerned with the second of these conditions.

Available Materials and Equipment

Most of the reading books, apparatus, and equipment published during the past twenty or thirty years, whether based on a Look and Say or a phonic method, appear to have been produced on the assumption that the teacher would instruct. On the other hand, in recent years the movement towards greater freedom in primary education has been reflected in certain changes in publications — for example, the production of simple picture dictionaries, reference books, and supplementary story books and a marked increase in the supply of well-produced, well-illustrated books for library corners.

However, one of the strongest trends in publications in the past ten years or so has been towards structured materials of varying kinds. This trend was seen in a reemphasis on phonics in the publications in England of, for instance, Daniels and Diack (1957), Southgate and Havenhand (1960), Stott (1962), and Reis (1962). The current interest in linguistic approaches to reading must be counted as part of this trend as should such publications as Sullivan's Programmed Reading (1963) and the S. R. A. Teaching Laboratories (Parker and Scannell 1963); all of which represent imports from the U. S. A. The experiments with programmed learning and the use of simple teaching machines for reading also illustrate the movement towards structure. The work of Moore (1963) in creating what he terms "an autotelic responsive environment", in the form of a talking electric typewriter, has also aroused some interest in England, where there are now two of these machines. Similarly, the introduction of simplified and regularised codes, such as i. t. a. (Downing 1962); colour codes, e. g., Gattengo (1962) and Jones (1967); or systems of diacritical marks, e. g., Fry (1964), all represent attempts to introduce structure into the reading environment.

In England, however, many progressive educationists and infant teachers who favour informal and active methods of learning for children have tended to regard structured media, materials, and equipment with suspicion, in the belief that their use might herald a return to formality of instruction. In certain instances these teachers' fears are justified. For example, with regard to media, the published materials for both Gattengo's (1962) "Words in Colour" and Jones' (1967) "Colour Story Reading", require substantial doses of teacher instruction. In contrast, i. t. a., with a greater variety of published materials available, does lend itself more easily to discovery methods.

Linguistic approaches to reading and certain of the phonic schemes are also heavily teacher orientated. But in the field of phonic training it is equally possible for the materials to favour either teacher-instruction or pupil-learning. Stott's (1962) "Programmed Reading Kit", for instance, while advocating a small amount of teacher instruction and guidance, relies mainly on children learning by active methods in small groups or pairs by games and apparatus which are self-checking.

It is also clear that many of the principles relating to programmed learning and teaching machines are in accord with the beliefs of teachers in modern infant schools. One would imagine that these teachers could not fail to support such ideas as individualised learning and pacing, immediate diagnosis and correction of individual errors, low gradients of difficulty for slow learners, the personal participation of the learner, and the child's assumption of responsibility for his own learning and his independence of the teacher. Yet many progressive infant teachers have shown little interest in these ideas. It may be partly on account of expense, but probably it is that such innovations are regarded, often mistakenly, as representing formalised instruction.

Structuring Materials for Learning

It is not always realised that the meticulous planning of a framework for learning to read does not have to be accompanied by formalised instruction. In fact, the reverse is true: the more informal the classroom regime, the more it becomes imperative that the reading environment should be so structured as to not only encourage reading but to facilitate it.

In the quest for structured reading materials, one should, first, examine carefully all new media for beginning reading in the light not only of how they simplify and regularise the written code but of how best they can be utilised for learning rather than instructional situations. Any regular medium which eliminates the necessity for children to approach words in two different ways, that is both as irregular words to be learned by sight and as regular words which can be sounded, should encourage individual learning. The less complicated the code, from a printing point of view, the more likely it is that a sufficient variety of materials will be published to make active ways of learning possible.

Second, one needs to examine books and all other reading equipment with an eye to both the content and the required procedures. The content should be so planned as to facilitate child-learning, while the procedure for mastering the content should necessitate the child's being active rather than merely represent the teacher's exhausting herself to achieve small returns from the children. It might be suggested that five-minute teacher guidance and instruction and fifteen-minute pupil activity are more appropriate than if these figures are reversed.

If reading begins with a Look and Say method, the first books the child handles should be such that the teacher does not have to put each word into the child's mouth and repeat this procedure ad nauseum until the words have been learned by rote. If the teacher is to step down from this role of permanent prompter, the illustrations in the book should be so simple, unambiguous, and appropriate that the words printed on the page are those which will spring immediately to the child's mind. In addition, the structure underlying the build-up of words from page to page should be such as to lead the child inevitably and successfully forward. Many well-known Look and Say reading schemes are deficient in this respect so that the child must rely very heavily on the teacher's instruction and guidance, in the early stages.

The teacher who decides to begin reading with phonic training will find that most phonic reading schemes cannot be used without a large proportion of teacher instruction in the initial stages, although in the later stages minimal teacher guidance can lead to considerable amounts of learning in the form of pupil-directed activities. If, however, phonic training is introduced after the initial stages of a Look and Say approach, it is possible to find published apparatus, games, equipment, and supplementary workbooks which represent active learning situations for children.

Structuring the situation for beginning reading in progressive infant classes towards child learning rather than teacher instruction should, in the writer's view, go further than a consideration of simplified media and the selection of appropriate reading materials and equipment. It requires the skilful pre-organisation by the teacher of a considerable proportion of the reading materials within the classroom before children's free choice becomes operative.

The growing practice in many infant classes of making available to children a large, miscellaneous collection of books of varying levels of difficulty, however attractive or stimulating or useful they may appear, does not seem to be sufficient in itself to predetermine the acquisition of reading skill. Once motivation to learn to read is aroused, not only are small amounts of instruction valuable but graded practice is also necessary. This activity can best be arranged by ensuring that, at every stage, a child can be guided to choose books and equipment from a selection appropriate to his level of attainment. Freedom for the child to try to read materials which the teacher knows to be too difficult for him represents merely a frustrating situation, whereas subtle arrangements made by the teacher to ensure the child's inevitable success with the books he chooses to read represent the most useful freedom for individual learning.

Conclusions

The advantages to be gained, when the emphasis in beginning reading is on pupil learning rather than teacher instruction, are so great that one should continue to explore this line of development, which can be seen to be working well in certain British infant schools. Even so, children's initial reading progress will be facilitated by careful structuring of the total reading environment. In order to create an ideal learning situation, one needs to consider the use of regularised media, select materials and equipment of every kind which will lend themselves to heuristic methods of learning, and organise the arrangement of all the materials in such a way as to ensure the child's graded progress without sacrificing the motivation engendered by freedom of choice.

REFERENCES

 1. Daniels, J. C., and H. Diack. *The Royal Road Readers.* London: Chatto and Windus, 1957.
 2. Department of Education and Science. *Children and Their Primary Schools. Volume 1: The Report.* London: H. M. Stationery Office, 1967.
 3. Downing, J. A. *To Be Or Not To Be.* London: Cassell, 1962.
 4. Fry, E. "A Diacritical Marking System to Aid Beginning Reading Instruction", *Elementary English,* May 1964.
 5. Gattengo, C. *Words in Colour.* Reading: Cuisenaire, 1962.
 6. Jones, J. K. *Colour Story Reading.* London: Nelson, 1967.
 7. McNally, J., and W. Murray. *Key Words to Literacy.* London: Schoolmaster Publishing, 1962.
 8. Melser, J. *Read It Yourself Books.* London: Methuen, 1966.
 9. Moore, O. K. *Autotelic Responsive Environment and Exceptional Children.* Hamden, Connecticut: Responsive Environments Foundation, 1963.
10. Parker, D. H., and C. Scannell. *S.R.A. Reading Laboratories — Primary Reading Laboratory.* Chicago: Science Research Associates, 1963.
11. Reis, M. *Fun with Phonics.* Cambridge: Cambride Art, 1962.
12. Southgate, V., and J. Havenhand. *Sounds and Words.* London: University of London Press, 1960.
13. Southgate, V. *First Words.* London: Macmillan, 1968.
14. Stott, D. H. *Programmed Reading Kit.* Glasgow: Holmes, 1962.
15. Sullivan, M. W. *Programmed Reading.* Maidenhead: McGraw—Hill, 1963.
16. Taylor, J., and T. Ingleby. *Reading with Rhythm.* London: Longmans, 1961.

G. Srinivasachari

S.I.T.U. COUNCIL OF EDUCATIONAL RESEARCH
ROBERTSONPET, RAJA ANNAMALAIPURAM
MADRAS, INDIA

Selection of Words and Structures for Readers

WHAT IS LANGUAGE? Traditionalists and linguists define language in various conflicting ways, and it is here proposed to avoid the controversy. For the purpose of this paper, the lexical meaning of *language* is enough, interpreted here as words, phrases, and expressions especially used by authors in preparing reading materials for children. To this definition, however, may be added the expression of thoughts and feelings in words, which the dictionary lists separately; for experience shows that this aspect, more than any other, creates and sustains the child's interest in reading.

The terms *words* and *structures* need some explanation. *Word* is here defined as a sound or combination of sounds or its written or printed symbols used as a unit of language. According to Fries, words form a centre of interest for teacher and pupil and are the first body of material to be taken into consideration in any method of language study. Advocates of the Look and Say and Sentence Method of teaching reading may not accept this view.

Kinds of Words and Structures. Now *words* in the title of this paper means language units both spoken and written and belonging to both the categories of structure words, called *empty* by some linguists, and content words, called *full* words.

An explanation is perhaps needed for the use of *structure.* Its use with reference to language has now become common, and linguists prefer structure to grammar. The notion of levels of linguistic structures is found in the work of J. R. Firth and his colleagues. Based on this, Barbara Strang mentions three levels of structure — namely, phonological, grammatical, and lexical — admitting that the middle one dovetails into the first and the third.

Structure means something that is built. A sentence, in spite of two hundred or more different but not quite satisfactory definitions, is essentially a constructed unit of language. Patterns so constructed are here called structures. Although there are many dialects and some differences between British English and American English, the kernal sentences which form the basis for

80

transformation through subordination, expansion, substitution, and inversion are the same wherever English is spoken. Nida (1) dealing with contrasting features of structural outlines says, "By the structure we mean the morphemes and combination of morphemes described according to their classes and in terms of their pertinent environment, i.e., by immediate constituents". This connotation of structure does not, in the writer's opinion, differ fundamentally from the syntactical relationship of words in the grammar of the traditionalist.

The Situation of Teaching and Learning English in India

The situation obtaining in India may be briefly stated: The curriculum (syllabus) in English consists of a list of essential words and a list of teaching items (structure words and sentence patterns). The procedure adopted in teaching is described as the *Structural Approach.* The duration of the course in English varies from four to nine years in the different states.

Teachers and authors are at liberty to alter the prescribed vocabulary to the extent of 10 percent of the total number of words, ranging from about 1,000 to 2,000. The teaching items are mandatory. Words, phrases, and sentence patterns contained in the teaching items are graded according to certain principles, chiefly from the point of view of difficulty in learning. The comparatively easy structures come first. Thus, the teaching of English is governed by the controlled vocabulary and graded structures. Books for detailed and non-detailed study must be in strict conformity with the syllabus laid down.

It was in 1952 that a standardized structural syllabus with controlled vocabulary came into force first in Madras and then in the other states. Within a few years, for some reason or another, alternative gradings were brought out in Madras; and at present in almost all the states in India, English as a second language is taught through some kind of structural approach and controlled vocabulary.

Yet, one is at present confronted with a gap between the school final level of English and that expected at the entrance to a university. For the past two years the S. I. T. U. Council of Educational Research has been trying to identify the areas of deficiency and work out schemes to bridge the gulf. The results of tests administered show that a large percentage of students, after completing their education, have no understanding of the sentence unit. Most of them who pass out of the secondary schools have not read any book other than the textbook prescribed for detailed study because graded reading books have not been made available in sufficient number and variety.

The Purpose of This Paper. The main purpose of this paper is to place before the Second World Congress on Reading the selection of words and structures for readers of English as a second language, according to views based on the writer's experience and knowledge as teacher and author.

When there was no prescription for controlled vocabulary or graded structures, the authors of readers chose words and sentence patterns according to the need and the ability of learners of particular age groups. The choice was to a considerable extent impressionistic rather than objective. In modern methods of teaching language, either as mother tongue or as a second language, the selection of words and structures is based on objective considerations more than before.

Criteria for Selection of Words

According to Fries the assumption that skill in a language must begin with words most commonly in use led to the counting of words and the establishment of the frequency series. But the fact seems to be quite the contrary. Frequency lists led to the development of skill in language with words commonly in use.

The Contribution of Fries. It is not possible to summarize the attempts at vocabulary selection in English. One cannot be too grateful to Charles C. Fries for his *English Word Lists,* a book which is an objective survey of the principal word lists in English. His notes on "Seven English Word Lists" are very useful to those interested in vocabulary selection. They are *Basic English* by Ogden; *Definition Vocabulary* by West; *Standard English Vocabulary* (the 100-word radius) by Palmer and Hornby; *The Teachers' Workbook* by Thorndike; *Interim Report on Vocabulary Selection* by a committee composed of Faucett, Palmer, Thorndike, and West; *Words with Values 1 to 34* by Faucett and Maki; and *Little English* by Aiken.

Fries advises that in the selection of words, basic English is sound with its list of 600 "things", 200 of which are *picturable* and 150 of which are *qualities*. Basic English has only eighteen chosen "operators". The argument that the "learning weight" is considerably reduced when the number of verbs is limited is not quite tenable, for the number of senses in which each of the operators is used in combination with prepositions has to be taken into account. Consider, for example, the subtle differences in meaning of idiomatic turns such as *get at, get to,* and *get on* which add to the learning load.

One has to count separately the number of phrases and idioms which can be formed by the use of each operator for estimating the learning load. Whether an idiom made by the operator in combination with other words is really easier than having a separate word with the same meaning has to be investigated. Further, to say to a learner, as basic does, "Thus far, and no further" is arbitrary and discouraging. Again, as Fries says, "the passing from such a limited vocabulary and basic grammar to the understanding of normal English and later, if desired, to the productive use of normal English, is a path beset with difficulties". The expressions "productive use" and "receptive use" should be interpreted according to the need of the learner.

So far as the teaching of English in India is concerned, for several decades to come, there will be need for both uses. The immediate need is the receptive, for a great deal of translation from English or other European languages has to be done by scholars to make the principal languages of India attain that flexibility necessary for absorbing and transmitting modern scientific, political, and economic thought. The productive use is necessary for establishing fruitful cultural contacts with the developed countries of the world. Effective use of English is necessary to rouse in the developed countries an interest in the socioeconomical problems of India. Books and journals necessary for communication as well as for improvement of Indian languages can, for several years to come, be had only in English. Learners of other European languages are far too few in number.

Some Factors Requiring Adequate Attention

Control of vocabulary material in the early reading books is no doubt essential; but if this control is added to, the textbook material may not sustain the interest of the child in reading. It must be realised that children increase their vocabulary and improve their sentence structure not by studying one reading book in minute detail but by reading many books. Therefore, plenty of graded reading material should be provided.

To insist that even the supplementary readers should be in the controlled vocabulary and in the structures already taught is, in a way, harmful to the child's development of reading interest. In learning language through adult contact, the child meets with situations when what is spoken is beyond his comprehension. What does the child do then? If he is not interested, he is indifferent. If he is interested, he takes pains to find out the meaning. The natural way is to let an expression unfold its meaning gradually to the child. The reading material, particularly that which is meant for supplementary reading, should provide such situations as would promote self-help in understanding.

In a Tamil grammar of the early centuries of the Xian Era, there is a *sutra* which says that grammar is like the oil pressed out of the ginger seed. If there is no seed, there is no oil; similarly, if there is no literature, there is no grammar. This statement means going to literature first and then to grammar.

The writer is a firm believer in the necessity of teaching grammar of the descriptive kind, but in his scheme this study comes only after acquainting children with patterns in interesting and meaningful contexts, both oral and written.

Will a complete course in syntax by itself ensure permanent interest in reading worthwhile books and journals in English? Probably not. But the course will be useful for the application of syntactical rules after a good deal of reading has been done.

Some Dichotomies. A great deal of harm has been done to language teaching and learning by a rigid adherence to some dichotomies. The distinction between form and meaning has already been referred to. It is said that language is a skill subject, not a knowledge subject; this approach often means emphasis on reproducing structures carrying nothing to stimulate the thought of the child.

Another dichotomy is the distinction between language and literature. Shakespeare and Milton may rightly be kept out of sight of the learners. But modern prose pieces and simple poems that touch the heart and the imagination of children should not be denied to them.

Those who have written books that are considered classics have all been gifted men and women who have by their works delighted millions of children throughout the world. To keep children from such books too long, in the name of scientific grading, is not doing the right thing by children.

Suggestions. It is suggested that the word list in second language may contain only the structural words, leaving it to teachers and authors to distribute them suitably among the different standards. The meanings in which each structural word can be used should be indicated through illustrative sentences. Perfect liberty may be given to authors to choose content words according to the environmental needs. It is not desirable to nationalise textbooks in language. When it is nationalised, a single series of readers for both rural and urban areas will not do. There must be at least three or four parallel sets of readers to suit different environments.

As for the structure list, it is enough if only the kernel structures are listed, stating the period necessary for processing them. In English, the pattern — subject-verb-object or complement with its variations in negation, interrogation, and exclamation — has to be given dire importance. The enlargement of the *subject/object* (extension of verb) by word, phrase, or clause should also be indicated. Both analysis and synthesis should be practised. The tense forms and their uses should also be systematically introduced. A specific number of phrases with illustrative sentences should be given. Provision for plenty of graded reading materials should be made in the early standards so that the transition to standard English books may be rendered as easily and rapidly as possible.

What S.I.T.U. Council has done for Tamil

Very few Indian languages have developed word lists for readers. The National Council of Educational Research and Training, New Delhi, with the aid of a team of experts from Columbia University evolved principles for the selection of words and structures in Hindi. Constance M. McCullough's monograph enunciating principles and procedures for designing early readers was perhaps the first of its kind in India.

The S. I. T. U. Council worked out a longitudinal project (1962—1967) of listing the functional vocabulary of preschool-age children (age group three to five). Trained observers recorded the whole utterances of children belonging to different socioeconomic levels. From these utterances words were taken out and listed according to certain areas. It was not possible to analyse all the 700 study sheets collected. Only 281 of them were analysed; for checking, the utterances of about 70 additional children of the Sabhesan Bala Brindhavan Nursery were tape recorded and studied.

Based on this study, two reports, an *Interim Report* and a *Final Report*, have been published. The main object of the study is to establish the need of preparing reading materials for Standard I which will be as near to the child's language and thought as possible and lay a strong and sound foundation for reading.

One hopes that it will be possible for the S. I. T. U. Council of Educational Research, Madras, to demonstrate by practical work the principles that should be applied for vocabulary selection, choice of sentence patterns, and thought content in the mother tongue of the early readers.

All schools of thought relating to language teaching agree that speech is the primary form of language which underlies all writing. It is also agreed that language patterns should be learned in the spoken language before they are introduced in the printed form. It is firmly believed that the vocabulary and sentence patterns commonly used by children should form the main basis for early reading material for primary school children. The process is, as Ruth G. Strickland observes, in a sense, the reverse of that in vogue.

Some explanation is perhaps necessary for the view that the language patterns already used by children should appear in the materials designed for the teaching of reading. In the first place, the vocabulary of the present-day children who react to the radio and cinema and use modern means of transport is wider than that of the children of the same age group forty or fifty years ago. Children are definitely acquiring language forms more rapidly today, presumably because of the latitude given to them for free expression both at home and at school.

In these circumstances, to reply mainly on written material for reading lessons would be unrealistic and dull; such material will not create reading interest in children. If the vocabulary and sentence patterns in the reading material are unrelated to those used by children, then children cannot react favourably. It is, therefore, urged that the language of early textbooks in Tamil should bear a reasonable relationship to that already in the possession of children. Only then can a sure foundation be laid to make language serve as the most effective instrument for the development of mental powers (2).

REFERENCES

1. Nida, Eugene A. *Morphology* (Second Edition). Ann Arbor: University of Michigan Press, 1957, 22.
2. Functional Vocabulary of Preschool Children (Final Report). The S.I.T.U. Council of Educational Research, Madras, 18, 30-31.

Chinna Chacko

USAID
RABI BHAVAN
KATHMANDU, NEPAL

Production of Reading Materials: A Comparative Study

ONE OF THE important steps in achieving the worthy aim of this conference — Reading, a human right — is the provision of right reading materials. Two years ago the writer related the problem of providing reading materials for children in India while Rajguru described the attempts made in India to make reading a human right for adults. At that time the writer was working on the reading project of the National Council of Educational Research and Training. This project has produced the first graded reading series and related instructional materials in India.

Since April 1968 the council has granted the writer a special leave to work with the Education Division of AID for preparing similar reading materials for Nepal.

It is felt that the general approach and most of the steps taken in developing a balanced reading program in India have been very effective. This same approach may work well in other newly developing countries. In Nepal, as in India, it has been necessary to plan very carefully so that with the minimum resources available one could get the maximum benefit.

Schools in Nepal

It wouuld not be inappropriate here to acquaint the reader with Nepal's current educational system and the present status of the reading materials.

Up to 1951 there were only 200 primary schools, 21 high schools and only one college in the whole of Nepal. The 1966—1967 report from the Ministry of Education shows that at present there are 5,640 primary schools, 243 high schools, 29 colleges, and one university in Nepal. The *primary* progress is phenomenal, and yet it is still inadequate for the purposes because this number takes care of only 28 percent of the primary school population — still a long way off from the goal of free and compulsory education for all. Except in forty-five villages and panchayats (the local elected governing body), primary

87

education is not free. Again, as in many countries with similar problems, the quality of education has not kept up with the quantitative improvement.

According to the same report, of the 13,400 teachers presently employed, 10,000 teachers are untrained. These untrained teachers have at the most seven years of schooling and many have only about five years. The other 3,000 teachers have had ten years of schooling and one year training in a normal school.

The physical conditions of 90 percent of the classrooms in Nepal are far from satisfactory. Often they have no windows; a small door is the only source of ventilation. The number of children in one classroom ranges anywhere from sixty to one hundred. There are no audiovisual materials nor even a chart in the classrooms, and often even a blackboard is a luxury. Most of the children as well as the teachers outside the Kathmandu Valley do not even have textbooks. Because there are no roads, books cannot be distributed.

There is a great dearth of trained teachers in Nepal. Their salaries are very low, and the teaching conditions are very poor. Out of the 5,000 schools, 2,000 are one-teacher schools. Another two thousand have two teachers. The remaining have more than two teachers. More than 4,000 schools have up to five grades. Out of the 182,000 children in class, only 80,000 — a little less than half — go to the second grade, and only 33,000 reach the sixth grade.

In all there are thirty distinct languages spoken in Nepal. These belong to the two main families — Indo-aryan and Tibeto-Burman.

There are various levels of speaking the Nepali language, just as in Hindi; but Nepali has four to five levels compared to the three levels in Hindi — one level being used for speaking to younger persons and another, to people below oneself in status, then between equals, between people who are older and above one's status, and to the king and the royal family members (eg-shri Panch Sarkar and parents is six sarkar). Now the Indo-Burman language speakers (Newaris, Gurund's) do not have this distinction; and so when they learn the language, they face a set of problems that are different from the problems faced by speakers of the Indo-aryan language. Apart from the confusion and difficulties it creates in learning the correct sounds, the Tibeto-Burman speakers have a greater problem of learning the different forms of language.

Fortunately linguists studying these specific problems are providing a source of help in the construction of exercises and other aids. These will be included in the textbook and the manuals.

The first Nepal government language series was published in 1964. The fact everything — even paper and ink — has to come from outside Nepal makes printing very costly. There are some available books of uncertain quality produced by private publishers. Although the government publications are a great improvement over the others, still these publishers are far from satisfactory. Often the same topic and lesson with very little change are repeated in two or three successive textbooks. The presentation lacks variety, and even in grade seven only three forms of writing are used — story, narrative, and poem. The words are controlled in these textbooks, but in each lesson the number of words varies greatly. There is no gradation either of content, language, or vocabulary. No provision is made for the teaching of reading skills. A manual accompanies a textbook but is of little help. Usually all the new words are listed, but no suggestions are given as to how to teach the words. One lesson recommends the teaching of twenty-one letters, a number which is a little less than half of the whole letters of the Nepali alphabet!

There is little coordination of work among the agencies working in education; and, unfortunately, because of this lack there is a duplication of work which Nepal can ill afford.

What is being done in Nepal to remedy this situation? Because of the time limitation, only the preparation, production, and distribution of reading materials for primary schools in Nepal will be discussed.

Preparation of Reading Materials

The first step was to plan a balanced reading program for Nepal. Now, we are attempting to coordinate all the possible resources and to eliminate all the duplication of effort already mentioned.

A high level committee has formed with representatives from each of the following agencies — His Majesty's Government, Educational Materials Center; staff from the Teachers College and linguists and educators from Tribhuvan University; staff from the Normal School; teachers from private schools; teachers from laboratory school; free lance writers; UNESCO; and United States Agency for International Development.

The functions of this committee are to coordinate all the resources — financial, technical, and educational; to evaluate and give guidance on the prepared plan for the development of the balanced reading program; to assign duties to various agencies; to check the progress of each project; to provide for the production, publicity, and distribution of all the materials prepared; to fix the remuneration for the different types of work; to appoint a coordinator to supervise and direct various efforts; and to appoint other personnel as the need arises.

The coordinator will be a member of the high level committee with responsibility for drawing up the programs, guiding the individual projects, and getting the necessary assistance by interpreting the needs of each of the projects to the committee and securing help.

Help Underway

Three work areas have been selected for immediate attention: 1) research and testing, 2) preparation of educational materials, and 3) teacher education.

A subcommittee composed of representatives from these three work areas has been established to assist the coordinator. The special function of this committee is to draw up a long-range program for each of the three work areas, to establish priorities, to make time targets, and to supervise specific projects.

In *research and testing*, the following projects have been undertaken, and the preliminaries are being done now. Lecturers from normal schools and training schools are in charge of each project with the help of graduate students and part-time assistants.

1. Studies on readiness. The first drafts of an auditory discrimination test have been drawn and illustrations are being prepared. In a week's time the pilot study will be conducted. Work on visual discrimination tests are in progress.

2. Studies on vocabulary. To find the hearing and spoken vocabulary, the results of these studies will guide the writing of the textbooks. The designs for these studies are being prepared at Teachers College.

3. A pilot study. A pilot study on spelling has been conducted. Two hundred and fifty second graders from different schools were tested. Out of the thirty words given, the highest score was twenty and the frequency was two. The study revealed, too, that there were many letters of the alphabet many children did not know. Also, the special difficulties encountered by children who speak a different language at home were defined.

   Plans are being made for a comprehensive study so that more specific help can be given in listening, speaking, and writing. As Nepali is a highly phonetic language, specific training can help to make children almost perfect spellers.

4. A fourth study undertaken with the help of the linguists of the university is to find out the specific problems involved in learning Nepali by all children who speak a different tongue at home. This study is urgent because although Nepali is considered as the mother tongue, only 10 to 30 percent of the whole population speak the language. And in different parts of the country, where an entirely different language is spoken even the teachers do not know Nepali although they are required to teach it. Whether the language is gurung' or sherpa there is only one language reader and that is Nepali. Consequently, Nepali is taught in the language of the area in which the school is situated. Other studies have been planned; but because of the shortage of manpower, one has to keep them aside at present.

Package Programmes

Because of the poor condition of the school and the lack of the trained teachers, it was decided to prepare a package programme consisting of the following materials to be given free to every teacher. Helicopters will be used to distribute these materials because travel by road is impossible at present. USAID, UNESCO, and His Majesty's Government will bear the expenses.

Included in each package will be syllabus, a set of graded readers, and manuals to accompany each textbook. The manual will give specific help to meet the difficulties of teaching and learning a second language along with specific instructions as to how to teach each lesson. These manuals will be interleaved with text pages. To cut down the cost of production, the text pages will be in black and white.

Included in the package also will be a reading readiness kit with charts, flannelgraph, and flash cards for developing the various skills required to read Nepali successfully.

Workbooks are also a definite part of the package programme. For Nepal these are a necessity because they not only help the child develop specific skills but also help the teacher. These workbooks are the one written record of the child's achievement. Of course, care would be taken that these workbooks will not be merely given as an exercise book to pass time when the teacher is busy.

A set of supplementary readers is also included in the package programme. These readers will provide an opportunity for children to practice their reading and to discover the joy between the covers of the book. Also included is a set of stories graded for each age and grade. Except for the great epics *Ramayana* and *Mahabharat* even the *Pancha Tanthra* is not widely known to the teachers.

One may rightly wonder how all these things are going to be done. Apart from the writer at Educational Materials Center, the teachers in lab schools, lecturers from teachers college and normal schools, free lance writers, and interested and able housewives are all a party to this joint endeavour. While one group is busy drawing up the content, writing, checking, and rewriting selections for books, another group is selecting and making available all the resources and materials; and a third group is working on the anthology for the teachers.

Work Underway in Teacher Education. Plans for teacher education are as follows: 1) improving the preservice training curriculum, 2) preparing programmed and other materials for training the 10,000 untrained teachers, and 3) preparing a group of resource personnel and specific plans for conducting special in-service training courses.

In Nepal teachers do not have even initial training, and so the number of teachers capable of leading a workshop is very limited. But the present plan is to train all the teachers in the five normal schools scattered around the country. These teachers will then conduct the special in-service training courses. The writer is happy to say that one has the marvelous assistance of the teach corps in this endeavour and, in fact, the first such workshop is being conducted now. A few hint about the specific problem of language instruction and of preparing language in Nepal textbooks.

Concluding Statement

This programme may sound like a very ambitious programme for Nepal. True, it is both ambitious and difficult. But the work is planned in such a way that one can attack several problems simultaneously. Even though this programme cannot be accomplished in one or two years, one does expect each year to show a steady advance toward the final goals. To make reading a human right the people working in this area in Nepal are determined to go ahead till the goal is achieved.

PROGRAMS: SEARCHING AND SELECTING

Ethel M. King

UNIVERSITY OF CALGARY
CALGARY, ALBERTA
CANADA

Organization of Reading Programmes

The success of the total reading programme may be likened to a wheel revolving around the teacher, the hub. To insure a smooth, uninterrupted journey many spokes are needed. These spokes are the skills of reading which become stronger with each succeeding year. The thumpety-thump of uneven growth or the squeaking of unused parts causes a rather unpleasant ride for some children. Finally, the organization provides the rim on which the programme keeps rolling forward.

The major concern in planning and organizing reading programmes should be that of creating a learning environment which will facilitate progress in the reading achievement of all pupils. At all times in the development and evaluation of a programme, it is important to retain this emphasis on the progress of individuals, rather than on the mechanics of the organizational pattern.

Kinds of Organization

Generally, one of three major approaches to organizing reading instruction is emphasized: the organization of a reading programme on a schoolwide basis, the organization of a reading programme on a classroom basis, or the organization of a reading programme on an individualized basis. Proponents of each of these approaches claim to be individualizing instruction, although the methods used are somewhat divergent. The organization of a schoolwide reading programme has been largely on the basis of horizontal or vertical homogeneous grouping by reading ability. Horizontal homogeneous grouping or intraclass grouping has been used in large schools having more than one classroom of pupils of approximately the same age or grade level. Reading achievement groups are established within each grade level or chronological age group, either as a class assignment for the year or for scheduled reading periods only. In vertical homogeneous grouping or interclass grouping, pupils are moved to an assigned reading achievement group, irrespective of chronological age or grade level assignment. Obviously, the use of the word homogeneous in each of these schemes is inappropriate. In other than a one-to-one situation between teacher and pupil, no group can be truly homogeneous. Within self-contained classrooms, a great variety of organizational plans has been used including such types as achievement grouping, interest grouping, special needs grouping, and tutorial grouping or team learning. Different plans to organize reading programmes on either a classroom or on a schoolwide basis evolved because of the belief that grouping was desirable and necessary to reduce the range of reading abilities.

To promote the individualizing of instruction even further, some teachers have adopted the individualized reading approach. This approach stresses the self-selection by the pupils of the materials to be read. Instruction is provided mainly through pupil-teacher conferences and to a lesser degree through small groups established for a brief time for a single, specific purpose.

The research evidence is not clear on the relative effectiveness of each of the major approaches to organizing a reading programme Comprehensive, longitudinal studies are lacking, and the conflicting evidence from available studies which evaluate only a limited number of variables is difficult to assess. Nevertheless, assessing the degree to which an organizational plan facilitates the reading progress of individuals appears to be dependent on 1) the competency of the teacher, 2) the materials available for instructional purposes, and 3) the quality and use made of the diagnosis of each pupil.

New Developments

For each of these apparently crucial factors in an effective reading programme, new trends are emerging. In addition to the traditional methods of trying to improve teacher competency, some school systems are experimenting with team teaching. Materials of instruction are being expanded to include much more than books, and some of the new school libraries or instructional material centres reflect the changing emphasis. To focus attention on diagnostic teaching, some schools are providing for variations in the plans for advancing pupils through the school systems. These innovations are just three of the relatively new developments which have implications for organizational changes in reading programmes. Such innovations may function independently but are certainly not mutually exclusive. Again, research evidence is lacking, but with the increasing interest on reading programmes for children ages 8 to 14 it could well be that a number of much-needed studies will be generated.

Team Teaching. In a team-teaching situation two, three, or four teachers may assume responsibility for 50 to 100 pupils. The teachers plan cooperatively the content and method of instruction. Each teacher on the team assumes responsibilities congruent with his special competencies. Instruction using a variety of organizational patterns, procedures, and materials is possible. Small groups may receive instruction in specific skills, and instruction appropriate for a large group may also be included.

Certain values are claimed for the team-teaching situation. Teachers are stimulated to develop and refine their teaching procedures as plans are made cooperatively and methods of colleagues are discussed. Also, pupils are exposed to a variety of lessons and teacher personalities. While the amount of time required for planning is probably increased, this problem is compensated for by the reduction of individual planning and some released teaching time. One or more of the teachers on the team will have time to devote to helping individual pupils as needed. Just as there is a wide range of individual differences among pupils, there will also be a wide range of individual differences among teachers. A team-teaching situation would seem to have the best chances of strengthening a programme when participation of teachers is on a voluntary basis. Obviously, traditional architectural designs for schools are not suitable for team teaching. Newer schools are being designed imaginatively with large open areas for instruction. And in some of the older schools the "Battle of Jericho" rages, as "the walls come tumbling down".

Instructional Materials Centre. In newer schools or in modified existing structures, the emerging concept of an instructional materials centre provides challenging opportunities for the resourceful teacher. The instructional materials centre is sometimes referred to as a "library of learning resources" as it houses, in addition to books, such materials as films, filmstrips, pictures, charts, records, tape recordings, globes, and maps. To gain the maximum benefits from such a centre, the total school programme needs to be organized in such a way as to permit pupils to use the centre for independent study.

Continuous Progress Plans. Many schools are experimenting with variations in school progress. In North America, for many years a graded system has been used in schools. Between Canada and the United States there have been some practical differences in the so-called grade schools. In other countries different terminology and organizational patterns have been used, but there is a number of common basic principles. Essentially, school programmes were organized so that pupils were expected to complete, with a reasonable degree of mastery, a predetermined sequence of work in a prescribed period of time. This basis for organization is now being challenged.

An exhaustive survey of the variations in school and classroom organizations is not possible, but the programmes are known by names such as nongraded, ungraded, levels, continuous progress, and streaming.

The new programmes are an attempt to provide pupils with the opportunity to progress through school by having the instruction adjusted to the pupils' achievement, rather than by having the pupils try to achieve arbitrarily established standards. Obviously this plan is an oversimplification of the goals as new programmes are not necessarily the antithesis of traditional ones. Nevertheless, the innovations do reflect a changing emphasis in organizational patterns.

Implications for Reading Programmes

The implications of organizational changes are numerous for the reading programme specifically. The primary objective of a continuous or ungraded reading programme is to organize a flexible reading programme which provides instruction and materials most suited to the needs of a particular group of pupils. Implicit in the theory of this kind of organization for a reading programme is the availability of a great number of alternatives for teachers to adjust their reading programmes to the progress of the pupils. In practice, however, adaptability of instruction is related directly to the resourcefulness of the teacher and to the amount and kind of materials available.

The organization of reading groups is based on combined evaluations which include test results, teacher judgment, and in doubtful cases further evaluation by a reading consultant. After the initial evaluation teachers have the opportunity cooperatively to assign pupils to one of a number of groups according to each pupil's reading achievement and expected rate of progress. Following placement in small groups the pupils may be moved from one level to the next higher level or, if necessary, to a lower level for a short period of time. For children of a designated age range, different reading levels are established. For example, pupils ages nine to eleven might be assigned to one of ten to fifteen different reading levels.

A brief description of an ongoing programme illustrates even more specifically how organizational changes may affect the reading programme. One school uses team teaching in self-contained classrooms for the first three years and team teaching in the open-area facilities with no internal walls for the following three years. The school, accommodating 380 children, is equipped with an instructional materials centre. The staff consists of a principal, a vice-principal, fourteen teachers, a teacher librarian, a secretary, and a teacher aide.

Because of new kinds of facilities and organization within the school, the reading programme has been modified. In the open areas of instruction a variety of kinds of lessons might be running concurrently. Occasionally, all pupils might participate as one large group. At other times, one or more small group lessons might be taught by different teachers in different corners of the room. During a large portion of the reading period a varying number of pupils would be engaged in individualized reading activities. As needed, pupils move freely to and from the instructional materials centre. In addition to this highly planned but apparently fluid organization, a number of additional projects are pursued. For superior readers enrichment reading units utilizing a great variety of materials from the instructional materials centre are included from time to time. In addition, superior readers are responding well to an increased emphasis on speech, choral speech, plays, and literature appreciation by studying literary style and by listening to various literary forms on records or tapes. On occasion, pupil-team learning is implemented. Under a teacher-guided plan one pupil is paired with another, particularly for specific review lessons on skills. The additional practice is deemed beneficial for the weaker pupils and reinforces the skills for the better readers. Not only are skills of reading being presented in a greater variety of ways than previously but reports also indicate that pupils are reading much more extensively. The teacher librarian has initiated many new activities, such as, organizing reading clubs, conducting story hours, and planning with teachers for suitable reading activities in the content subject. One pupil from each reading group is trained to check out books for his group so that the librarian is freed from some of the time-consuming routine tasks in order to devote more time to professional activities.

Some other schools provide open-area instruction on certain occasions by folding or sliding walls of otherwise self-contained classrooms. In a sense greater flexibility in organizational patterns is, therefore, provided.

Special Problems in Programmes for Older Pupils

The development of reading programmes for pupils ages twelve to fourteen is more recent than for younger pupils. Generally, it is agreed that this age is a period for refining reading skills by learning to read effectively on an increasing number of topics from an increasing number of sources. No one would deny the importance of having a continuous programme; yet in almost all patterns of school organization, there is an interruption in developmental programmes which, in practice, can be shown to have a marked effect on reading instruction. In North America this situation usually occurs between ages eleven and twelve.

Currently for those schools which do provide reading instruction for this older group, ages twelve to fourteen, a variety of organizational patterns exists. Departmentalized instruction or teaching by subject specialists tends to be prevalent. The concern in this system is whether the rigid divisions in the school day impose restrictions which interfere with integrated learnings, particularly since reading does not have a content of its own but is a skill applied to the various subjects. In some schools special reading classes are taught "for those who need it". Such a programme will accomplish little in advancing the reading competency of all pupils. The range of individual differences will be extended with each succeeding year in a good programme. Therefore, it is essential that teachers are cognizant of these differences.

Some of the new developments discussed previously may have unique implications for more advanced pupils. Team teaching might include not only two to four teachers instructing a large number of pupils in varied reading activities but also a reading specialist teaming with a subject-matter specialist to develop a programme which strengthens the application of reading skills. As readers become increasingly efficient, then the availability of time and materials for independent study becomes extremely important. Instructional materials centres may continue to play a vital role in the education of the pupil. If progress in acquiring reading skill is to be continuous, then the system must make specific and direct provision for transmitting information on the achievement of each pupil from one teacher to another. Of even greater concern is the sharing of information when a pupil is transferred or "graduated" from one division of the school programme to another.

Conclusion

Organizational changes in reading programmes should be undertaken when there is some evidence that the changes will facilitate progress of the individuals. A good reading programme provides for the use of books on varied levels of reading difficulty. There should be large groups, small groups, and individual instruction. Skill development should be assessed at frequent intervals. Diagnosis of strengths and weaknesses should be recorded on an individual basis.

While research evidence has not been accumulated yet, some of the new developments are worthy of serious consideration. The organizational changes discussed are based largely on teacher cooperation in planning, on sharing materials and facilities, on communication among teachers, and on frequent diagnosis and appraisal. Hopefully, the children will benefit from a "smoother ride" with continuous progress.

REFERENCES

1. Figurel, J. Allen (Ed.). *Reading and Inquiry,* Proceedings of the International Reading Association, 10, 1965, 128—170.
2. Figurel, J. Allen (Ed.). *Vistas in Reading,* Proceedings of the International Reading Association, Vol. 11, Part 1, 1966 (Copyright 1967), 134—155.
3. Lust, A. "McKee School: An Experiment in Instructional Improvement", *C.S.A. Bulletin.* Edmonton, Alberta Teachers' Association, May 1968, 15—37.
4. Robinson, H. Alan. *Meeting Individual Differences in Reading,* Proceedings of the Annual Conference on Reading, Supplementary Educational Monographs, No. 94. University of Chicago Press, 1964.
5. Robinson, Helen M. *Reading Instruction in Various Patterns of Grouping,* Proceedings of the Annual Conference on Reading, Supplementary Educational Monographs, No. 89. University of Chicago Press, 1959.

Miles A. Tinker

991 WINTHER WAY
SANTA BARBARA, CALIFORNIA
UNITED STATES OF AMERICA

Selecting Methods for Evaluating Reading Progress

EVERY TEACHER should appreciate the fact that evaluating reading progress is closely tied with the instructional program. The teacher must discover the strengths and weaknesses of each child in order to adjust instruction to the needs of all pupils.

A major task of the teacher is the selection of methods to be used in evaluating reading progress. Both formal (standardized tests) and informal techniques are used to appraise a child's reading status, whether adequate or deficient. Such an appraisal will furnish the teacher with information to use in individualizing instruction.

To adjust a child's instruction in reading to his specific needs, it is necessary to evaluate his reading abilities at intervals, such as when he enters grade two and then as the program of instruction develops sequentially. There should be periodic measurements of reading ability, in addition to day-by-day observation and checking by the teacher. The techniques employed at any given time will depend upon what is to be appraised; i. e., one method may be more useful for evaluating skill in some aspect of word recognition, another for a specific study skill.

This discussion will be limited to use of standardized tests, informal reading tests, teacher observation, and records.

Standardized tests

Standardized tests are measuring devices of established reliability and validity. They furnish norms or standards of achievement for a specific series of school grades. Ordinarily these tests are readily scored, and usually the scores are easily interpreted by the teacher. When a standardized test is used, the teacher, through reference to the norms, can ascertain the grade level of a pupil or of a class.

Two general types of standardized reading tests are available. The survey tests, such as the Gates-Macginitie Reading Survey, are used primarily to ascertain a pupil's level of achievement in such basic reading abilities as vocabulary, comprehension, and speed. The diagnostic tests enable the teacher to discover a pupil's strengths and weaknesses in such specific skills as word perception, understanding sentences, and noting details. Some diagnostic tests, such as the Silent Reading Diagnostic Tests, are group tests; others, such as the Gates-McKillop Reading Diagnostic Tests, are highly specialized for diagnostic purposes.

To select a standardized test, the teacher should examine such lists as those given in Tinker and McCullough (5) and in the Sixth Mental Measurement Yearbook (2). After deciding which test or tests might be used, the school should obtain sample copies with manuals of directions of the tests selected for consideration. Items to consider in selecting a test are abilities to be measured, scope of grade levels, ease of scoring and interpreting scores, cost, and time length of testing.

The directions for administering a standardized test have been carefully designed so that the child taking the test can operate under the most favorable conditions for eliciting a valid measurement of his reading ability. And all published norms have been obtained under the conditions of use prescribed by the standard directions. Therefore, to make sure that the obtained scores are meaningful, it is necessary that the directions for administering the test be followed exactly as given. Any deviation from the standard directions will prevent a valid interpretation of the obtained scores.

Informal Reading Tests

The two most common kinds of informal reading tests are workbook tests and teacher-made tests. They are informal in the sense that they are not standardized. These tests are employed for the day-by-day appraisals needed in individualized teaching. The workbook tests are concerned largely with measurement of word identification and recognition skills, vocabulary, and comprehension. For the most part, such tests measure what is presently being taught in the accompanying basic program. An examination of the responses to the test items will frequently furnish important information on sources of reading difficulties so that prompt remedial measures may be taken.

Workbook tests measure success only with workbook materials which ordinarily cover only part of the tasks of any daily lesson. Therefore, the most satisfactory appraisal of daily progress can best be made by additional informal testing through use of tests made by the teachers themselves. The types of items in these tests are selected by the individual teacher. The make-up of the tests tends to approximate that in workbooks and standardized tests. Teacher manuals which accompany series of readers usually provide helpful suggestions for construction of test items.

Due to the manner of construction, teacher-made tests are readily adapted to checking daily, weekly, or monthly progress in learning. These informal tests reveal strengths and weaknessess of pupils and thus provide information for guidance in adjusting instruction to individual needs.

Informal oral reading tests are especially useful for guidance in reading instruction. A systematic informal measure of oral reading proficiency can be obtained readily by use of selections in a carefully graded series of basic readers, or one can use specially prepared test material such as Smith's Graded Selections for Informal Reading Diagnosis (3, 4). The teacher works with each child individually and notes his accuracy of pronunciation and degree of comprehension as he reads selections of increasing difficulty. Different levels of performance, as outlined by Betts (1), are readily ascertained by this method: level appropriate for extensive free reading, the instructional level, and the frustration level. The oral reading test can also furnish information useful in guiding day-by-day instruction. Analysis of the recorded errors will disclose individual needs by revealing inadequate use of verbal context, lack of skill in phonetic and structural analysis, and determination of whether the difficulty tends to arise at the beginning, middle, or end of words.

The use of the informal teacher-made tests makes it possible for the teacher to maintain intimate contact with each pupil's progress in learning to read.

Teacher Observation

Observation by the teacher of pupil behavior and pupil responses in the reading situation provides extremely useful information for appraising the pupil's growth in reading. This information, obtained by direct study of the child, is of great value as a supplement to the test results for following day-by-day proficiency in reading. The teacher can employ observation for more or less continuous appraisal of pupil success in learning what is being taught. The knowledge gained by such observation also provides a basis for whatever shifts in emphasis may be needed to meet individual needs.

Occasionally the teacher, to better understand a pupil, can make use of one or more personal conferences. Such conferences afford an opportunity to follow up leads derived from more general observation, to fill gaps with information not acquired earlier, and to strengthen the self-confidence of the child and his relationship to the teacher. Only by such direct observation can the teacher evaluate a variety of attitudes connected with reading which determine in large measure the child's readiness to make satisfactory progress. The teacher perceives signs of eagerness and joy with which the child approaches reading or the indifference or distaste which spells avoidance reactions. By such observations made at intervals any change in the child's attitudes towards the reading situation may be noted and used as a basis for modifying the instructional methods when indicated. Close watching also shows the teacher how proficiently the pupil employs study skills. For instance, he can note how effectively the pupil locates information and selects materials. Standardized tests cannot be expected to yield adequate evaluations of this sort. Though these informal measures of reading progress may lack objectivity, the able and experienced teacher can use them to advantage.

Records

It is not safe for any teacher to depend entirely upon memory for coordinating and appraising the strengths and weaknessess of the thirty or so individual children in his class. For this reason, he should keep records, preferably anecdotal and cumulative.

When the significant aspects of informal observation are noted in anecdotal form, the result is called an anecdotal record. These notations describe specific episodes or reactions to specific situations. For the most part, such anecdotes are concerned with reading situations or behavior related to reading. Although the anecdotes may later be employed in appraisal, they are at first written down merely as descriptions of incidents; for example, "John is now making real progress in combining verbal context clues with phonetic analysis when he identifies new words". A series of these notes may supply an important supplement to other observations and measurements used in appraising growth in reading.

When accumulated in usable form, certain data on a child constitute cumulative records. These data may consist of a teacher's records and observations, standardized test scores, anecdotal records, and data on strengths and weaknesses in one or another aspect of reading performance. When kept up to date, material in the cumulative record may be coordinated to evaluate patterns of behavior related to reading and to appraise growth in reading achievement. Especially valuable is the long-term pattern of behavior changes and reading development as revealed by cumulative records. In this pattern continuity and direction of growth in reading may be readily discerned.

In summary, one may note the following points in selecting methods for evaluating reading progress: 1) In choosing a standardized test, the teacher must decide what he wishes to measure, such as vocabulary knowledge or word recognition, and then select a test that has a sufficiently wide spread of possible scores and is a reliable and valid measure of the particular ability to be measured. 2) Sample copies of standardized tests should be obtained for inspection prior to ordering in quantity. The directions for administration should be checked for clearness and for ease of interpreting the obtained scores. The test chosen should be given by following the directions exactly as printed. 3) Informal teacher-made tests should be constructed carefully to measure what is being presently taught. 4) Oral reading tests should be carefully organized if taken from a series of basic readers, or tests already printed may be employed. 5) Both anecdotal and cumulative records should be well organized, dated, and kept up to date. 6) The results of measurement should be used to adjust instruction to individual needs of pupils.

1. Betts, E. A. *Foundations of Reading Instruction.* New York: American Book, 1957.
2. Buros, O. K. (Ed.). *The Sixth Mental Measurement Yearbook.* Highland Park, N.J.: Gryphon Press, 1965.
3. Smith, Nila Banton. *Graded Selections for Informal Reading Diagnosis, Grades 1 Through 3.* New York: New York University Press, 1959.
4. Smith, Nila Banton. *Graded Selections for Informal Reading Diagnosis Grades Four Through Six.* New York: New York University Press, 1963.
5. Tinker, M. A., and C. M. McCullough. *Teaching Elementary Reading* (3rd ed.). New York: Appleton—Century—Crofts, 1968.

Oliver Andresen

CHICAGO STATE COLLEGE
CHICAGO, ILLINOIS
and

Leonard Courtney

ST. MARY'S COLLEGE
WINONA, MINNESOTA
UNITED STATES OF AMERICA

Integrating Reading Instruction with Subject Matter

Among his many responsibilities a subject-matter teacher at the higher academic levels has three basic obligations. First, he must lead his students to an understanding of the important concepts of his specialty. Second, through classroom activities the teacher must help his students relate these concepts to the universe. In other words, students must be directed to apply the concepts learned in school to the solution of everyday problems. Third, the teacher must give instruction in the area of reading comprehension. Since reading is the process through which most learning is acquired, instruction in reading is imperative for successful understanding of the content being studied.

A basic complication in the fulfillment of these obligations is the range of differences among the students. Also, a teacher soon becomes aware of the variance of background among his students. How, therefore, can a subject-matter teacher design learning activities incorporating instruction for the enhancement of reading comprehension and background of experience? Also, how can he differentiate the difficulty of these activities in the light of his students' needs?

The learning activities grid

The purpose of this paper is to present a "tool" to aid the teacher in these tasks. This tool is a bilinear grid consisting of two axes. The vertical axis represents five levels of reading comprehension skills ranging from the literal level (the easiest) to the creative level (the most difficult). The horizontal axis represents the types of experiences to which a concept in a printed selection can be related. These types of experiences range from personal experiences (most familiar to the reader) to absolute experiences (least familiar to the reader).

Any learning activity involving reading can be plotted at a junction of a line from the vertical axis (reading comprehension levels) and a line from the horizontal axis (types of experiences). By plotting his learning activities on the grid, the teacher can assure himself that these activities include tasks enhancing both reading comprehension skills and background of experience. Also, he can differentiate the activities according to their degrees of difficulty. Using the grid in this manner will aid the subject-matter teacher in fulfilling his three basic obligations. (See Figure 1).

Figure 1. *Learning activities grid*

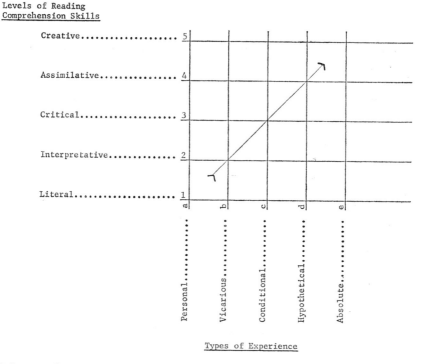

Types of Experience

The student

When a high school teacher contemplates the complexities of his profession, he should remember the confusion often experienced by his students. Not only must they learn new concepts, they must achieve this mastery during the most confusing years of their lives.

Perhaps the most sensitive representation of this adolescent dilemma is the statue of the little mermaid in the harbour at Copenhagen. The statue depicts Hans Christian Andersen's little mermaid who abandoned her home and family in the sea in order to win a handsome prince and an immortal soul. She did not win the prince; and at the end of the story her entry into paradise is left in abeyance for three hundred years. And so now she can be seen waiting on her rock, gazing nostalgically at the sea — her childhood home.

The little mermaid, of course, depicts more than a character in a fairy tale. It symbolizes the perplexities of all adolescents who must abandon childhood for the problems and responsibilities of the adult world.

To illustrate the use of the learning activities grid, therefore, let us assume that we are concerned with a high school literature class which is reading the story of Andersen's "Little Mermaid" as an example of an European classic for children.

Reading comprehension learning activities

Reading comprehension is primarily concerned with those skills by which the reader both understands and reacts to what the author is saying (2). These skills can be divided into five levels.

1. *Literal level.* At this level the reader recognizes and understands the author's stated ideas.

To enhance reading comprehension at this level, students should be directed to perform tasks requiring this level of understanding. A question requiring the recall, recognition, or knowledge of a stated fact in a reading selection would be this kind of task.

An example concerning the story "The Little Mermaid" would be the question: "Why did the mermaid wish to become a mortal?" In the story the mermaid is quoted as saying that she will do anything to win the handsome prince and an immortal soul.

2. *Interpretative level.* At this level the reader understands not only the stated ideas of the author but his implied ideas as well. In short, the reader sees implications or "reads between the lines".

A task requiring this level of understanding of reading material is the following question: "To become mortal the mermaid knew that she had to endure continual physical pain. And even then if the prince did not marry her, she would turn into foam on the sea. Yet, she chose to take this chance. Why?"

Although it is not stated in the story, the implication is strong that the little mermaid was willing to endure torment and the risk of death for a brief time as a mortal.

3. *Critical level.* At this level the reader understands not only the ideas, both stated and implied, but passes judgment on them in the light of his own experience.

A task requiring reading comprehension at this level calls for the evaluation of the author's thinking by the reader. This judgment must be supported by evidence within the selection. Following is an example of a question requiring this level of reading: "As the story ends, the mermaid does not marry the prince; yet, there remains the possibility of her immortality. Therefore, do you think her choice to become mortal was a worthy one?"

Here the student's opinion when reacting to the question is not so important as the logic he uses. The teacher, therefore, must challenge any reasoning by the student which is inadequate.

4. *Assimilative level.* At this level the reader not only understands, interprets, and evaluates the ideas in print but incorporates the valuable aspects of these ideas within his own thinking. In other words, the reader becomes a "coauthor" of an idea in print by combining it with thoughts from his previous experiences.

To read at this level the student must be able to analyze, synthesize, or trace the logic of a complex concept. Often he may need to do some research to comprehend what he reads at this level. An example of an assimilative level task would be to prepare a discourse on the theological implications in Andersen's "Little Mermaid".

5. *Creative level.* Creativity is generally recognized as the highest of all the higher mental processes. Reading at this level involves imaginative treatment of ideas, resulting in new insights, fresh ideas, and new organizations of thought.

Occasionally, after a particularly stimulating learning experience, a student is "set afire" with ideas for activities or projects of his own. If his ideas are sound, he should be given the opportunity to carry them out with as much independence as possible (*1*). An example might be a student's translating "The Little Mermaid" into a musical composition.

The relating of concepts to types of experience

A concept is not meaningful to a student until he applies it in terms of his own life. Such an application, educationally speaking, is an experience. Specifically, then, experience can be defined as the intellectual application of a concept to a given situation. Since experiential background is essential to comprehension, a student should learn to relate concepts he learns in the classroom to as many different types of experience as possible.

The writers of this paper have divided the range of experiences into five types. These types are defined according to their relevance to the reader.

1. *Personal experience.* The most relevant type of experience is first-hand. In order to recall a fact, interpret an idea, or criticise a concept, the student at least must draw upon first-hand experiences. Such an activity would be the relating of a concept to a personal experience. An example of a question calling

for this type of activity would be: "Explain your reactions to the story, 'The Little Mermaid' ". In responding, the student at least would draw upon his own opinions and feelings.

2. *Vicarious experience.* A vicarious experience is second-hand. When a student relates a concept he is reading to one he has heard of or has read about before, he is relating his learning to this type of experience. An example of a question calling for this type of activity would be: "Compare the fate of the little mermaid to that of Cinderella". Hopefully, by judicious questioning from the teacher, the student would realize that Cinderella was given her goals whereas the mermaid had to struggle for hers. Consequently, the story of the mermaid is a truer interpretation of life.

3. *Conditional experience.* When training a student's thinking processes, a teacher often adds a "condition" to reality. Questions beginning with "But what if . . ." or "Let's say that . . ." lead the student to relate a concept to a situation somewhat different from what he is accustomed. Such questions, therefore, lead him to relate a new concept to a conditional experience. An example would include the following: "What if the little mermaid had married the prince? Would the story be as effective as it is now?" Hopefully, the student could be led to realize that such a turn of events in the story would destroy its profound commentary about life.

4. *Hypothetical experience.* Again to encourage facility in thinking, a teacher occasionally will describe to the student an entirely new frame of reference or "universe" for the student to cope with. The new universe is an example of a hypothetical experience. A question calling for this type of experience is "Should a boy marry against his family's wishes even if it means his being disinherited?" Although a student's response will be an opinion, he should support it logically under the circumstances presented to him.

5. *Absolute experience.* Most sophisticated people recognize a "oneness" or central theme to the universe. Consequently, a student who has a thorough grasp of a new concept can see its relationship to many others. Seeing such relationships might, therefore, be termed as approaching absolute experience.

For example, let us say that a student in a class has worked for a scholarship at the price of great personal hardship. Yet, the scholarship is finally denied him because of his race, creed, or family status. His friends in the class, having understood the story "The Little Mermaid", would sense the suffering common to the mermaid and their disappointed friend. Consequently, rather than being unaffected by such an event, their minds would now be open with profound compassion to the student's suffering.

Conclusion

The grid, then, is to guide the teacher in the designing of learning activities for his subject-matter courses. By plotting the learning activities on the grid,

the teacher can assure himself that he is not neglecting tasks which will enhance the reading skills necessary for his course; nor will he neglect the skills
which will promote the students' relating of these skills to the problems of
their universe.

Also, although the class might be working on a single reading assignment,
all students need not be directed to perform the same tasks. Rather, students
may be grouped according to which point on the grid each one seems to perform at his best.

For example, during the reading of "The Little Mermaid", one group could
be answering a list of questions requiring literal responses related to the personal experience of reading the story (grid rating: 1a). Another group might
be directed to paraphrase the story in the style of James Thurber (grid rating: 2b). A third group might evaluate the story under the supposed condition that it had recently appeared in a teenage magazine (grid rating: 3c). A
few might study the life of Hans Christian Andersen and rewrite the story as
he might have written it today (grid rating: 4d). One or two students might
be launched on activities of their own design and within a frame of reference
of their own choosing. An example might be their writing a musical comedy
based on the story (grid rating: 5e).

Hopefully, then, by studying the story as subject matter, each student will
leave the story with understanding of concepts about life as seen through the
eyes of Andersen's genius. Also, hopefully, because of reading instruction, each
student will leave the story with better reading comprehension skills. Finally,
because of the enrichment of his own experiences, each student will leave the
story with a broader understanding of how to think about his own universe.
By this threefold growth he is, therefore, better prepared to meet the frontiers
of new learning yet to come.

REFERENCES

1. Andresen, Oliver. "An Experiment in Class Organization for High School Freshmen", in J. Allen Figurel (Ed.), *Improvement of Reading through Classroom
   Practice*, Proceedings of the International Reading Association, 9 (1964), 57.
2. Andresen, Oliver, and H. Alan Robinson. "Developing Competence in Reading
   Comprehension", in Marion D. Jenkinson (Ed.), *Reading Instruction: An International Form*, Proceedings of the First World Congress on Reading, Paris, France,
   1966. Newark, Delaware: International Reading Association, 1967, 99—107.

Nakorn Pongnoi

37 SUNNALUNG ROAD
CHIANG MAI,
THAILAND

Reading Centers in Remote Areas

IN THE JUNGLE MOUNTAINS of Northern Thailand, the lot of the hilltribe groups, numbering approximately 302,000 individuals, is a very grave one. These people differ from the Thai population in ethnic, cultural, and linguistic characteristics. Their livelihood was derived in the past from "slash and burn" farming of rice and opium. The Thai government has passed laws making this method of farming, cultivation, and sale of opium illegal. Without adequate Thai government assistance, the hilltribers can only wallow in destitution or return to their old but now criminal practices. A desire to raise these people to a more acceptable means of income stems not only from a humanitarian interest in their economic and civic welfare but also from a fear of antigovernment activities by an indigent people at odds with their government.

The hilltribes live in remote and difficult areas, almost inaccessible to anyone. Finally, the government of Thailand began to take an active part in the hilltribe problems, and, therefore, programs were instigated to help the hilltribers become economically sufficient by encompassing various aspects of a pressing social problem.

Today, the work is being done on a larger scale. Attention is being focused on three main problem divisions areas: education, resettlement, and occupational improvement. Obviously, the magnitude of the condition involving so many different types of people cannot be underestimated or ignored. What is necessary is the realization of the task.

In order to begin the massive effort, the government, working to a great extent through the Border Patrol Police, chose different types of strategies. The Thai government selected the Border Patrol Police, a unique and unusual agency for modernization, largely because it was the only Thai government presence in these remote areas. One strategy of this agency was the establishment of development centers in over sixty selected villages. In these areas are schools and agriculture centers in varying phases of development. Trained Thai college graduates, used as specialists, and the Border Patrol Policemen give advice and direction to the centers on such matters as improvement of crops, irrigation, education, animal husbandry, and sanitation. The Thai gov-

112

ernment has provided material to help in the form of agricultural and medical supplies, teaching aids, and building material. It was expected that the centers would succeed and flourish, under such a seemingly comprehensive and optimistic plan.

An Analysis of the Problem

These centers have proved unsatisfactory. Indicative of the unsatisfactory results is the inability to produce any amount of continuing activity to which the villagers will subscribe for any length of time. When the Border Patrol Policemen leave, the villagers usually return to their old practices — showing a lack of interest or care. In one village, the hilltribers did not prevent a cow from entering the school and eating portions of the teaching aids. Many hilltribers do not believe that the development centers are there for the villagers but rather for the good of the Border Patrol Police. These people feel suspicious of ulterior motives from the donors of assistance, because in hill tribe society where life is hard no one ever gives away anything for nothing, except on festival occasions. An example is their attitude toward the seeds and fruit trees given to them. They feel that these articles could not be too good, otherwise the Border Patrol Police would keep the articles for their own use!

Living as they do from day to day, hilltribers do not appreciate the value of long-range planning or training. They are overly critical if young fruit trees cannot produce within the span of a single season. A father of a boy who did not attend school asked the father of a school child, "What is the use of school attendance?" He pointed out that his child spent a profitable day hunting, while the schoolboy spent all day in a school just thinking about hunting.

There is always the "let-them-alone" attitude. For some tourists the condition of these people means more interesting subjects for photographing. For some research scholars these poor conditions mean unmarred research material, and for some government officers they mean no more headaches.

The cultural difference between the hilltribers and those sent to help them at development centers very often appears extreme. Time after time advisors and planners, no matter how well trained, seem to misjudge hilltribe reactions. Often the things that the planners think will be most welcomed and appreciated are ignored.

The hilltriber, on the other hand, experiences a feeling of inferiority when he comes in contact with Border Patrol Policemen or Thai specialists. The cultural and customary practices of the hilltribers, while valuable to him, can greatly impede his progress. For instance, a lot of hilltribers think that there is traditionally only one right way of doing things; new modern ways would cause calamity. The hilltriber finds security in supernatural things and longs for them as a point of relevance in his life. A person may walk as far as Hanoi, if somebody tells him that there is a god there. A whole village may pick up its belongings and leave because a bad omen such as a lame turtle limped into their village. The problems and obstacles are great — great enough to convince one that the effort of the development centers must be modified or the program will lead to failure. However, the welfare of the hilltriber, which determines to a great extent the security of Thailand, is so precious that a renewed effort must be made and the obvious causes of failure must be corrected.

The ideology behind the building of centers is basically sound, but oftentimes it does not work. Some mistakes are inevitable, since in most new projects trial and error must be used. One explanation of problems may be that the pride of the hilltriber is hurt. He feels that he should be able to give something in return for services rendered him. Maybe his intelligence, too, is often underestimated. When a Thai Government officer is insincere in his demonstration of good will or friendship toward the hilltribers, they can sense it. Sometimes anti-government agitators will enter a village and tell about evils, such as corruption in the government. In such a case, a counterexplanation should be given, not just a denial of its existence.

Reading for Adults — A Way to Solve Problems

An educational facet which has been ignored in the past in the development centers is that of teaching reading and writing to adults. The percentage of adult literacy in a hilltribe village is usually near zero; and if any one knows how to write, he most likely writes in Chinese. Foreign missionaries have done some work in adult education, but their efforts are often misdirected by teaching Thai in a Romanized alphabet or by teaching the hilltribe words using the Thai alphabet. It is most important that adult hilltribers learn to speak, read, and write in Thai. This type of learning prevents confusion and opens communication and understanding with other Thai people and with the government. Both the hilltriber and the Border Patrol Police would gain many benefits from such a program. If the Border Patrol Police teacher taught hilltribe adults in the evening and children in the day time, greater contact with the whole village would be gained. No longer would the task of influencing people be difficult, for teachers are always willing to converse with the people, even about the presence of agitators, since an established relationship has been set up. On the other hand, the hilltribers also would gain many things from this venture. Village children would stay in school because their parents would know something about the educational process and understand its value.

Respect and approval for the work that the Border Patrol Police is attempting might also be a consequence of such training. The role of the Border Patrol Police then would be better understood. Instead of appearing like someone who is an outside "snooper", a member of the police would become important in the villager's everyday life. Distrust about ulterior motives would vanish, and the overall welfare of the hilltriber, rather than only his security, would be secured.

Method

The task of getting adult hilltribers into a classroom seems impossible since they do not value things like distributed seeds or suggestions about irrigation and sanitation which may influence their daily life. The real reason that they do not appreciate education is that they have never seen it as being personally relevant. It is acknowledged that every man has a certain amount of pride and wishes to hold his head high among his fellow men. It is known that the poor man does not want to make any radical changes because he has never found anything rewarding — only backbreaking toil and endless drudgery. This situation can be applied directly to the education of the adult hilltribers. It would be useless to gather them all into a classroom and start teaching them the alphabet or fundamentals of Thai patriotism. That can come later. First, these people must be introduced to learning in ways immediately interesting and useful to them. Remember, they expect fast results.

A useful beginning approach to learning is first to teach the hilltribers how to read and write their names in Thai. They should see the usefulness of such a skill. A recognizable signature lends legitimacy to documents (such as bills of sale), contracts, and agreements. Research has been done on what is particularly interesting to the individuals of a certain village. If they like music and the playing of musical instruments, one starts by exchanging ideas about music with them. One teaches them how to read and write the names of instruments, then to read and write some simple songs. It is truly a joy to the hilltribers to see their beloved songs and poems in a written language!

Another approach is that of teaching reading and writing while working along with other developmental projects. For example, if seeds are distributed, rather than only giving them out with an explanation of what they are and how they are used, the Border Patrol Police teachers seize the opportunity to let the people read and write a little. On a seed package there is a picture of a tomato and easy and short directions. Experience has shown, after learning how to read, these people were more eager to plant the seed and to take better care of the plants. One can do the same with other equipment and tools. Sometimes one can teach hilltribers to write directions for their own references. This approach would be applicable to a handicraft program. A hilltribe handicraft sale center has been set up in town in the hope that this center will be a bridge between the hilltriber and lowland people. Hilltribers have a hard time remembering the details of an order, and so they ask to be taught how to write and read numbers, names of colours, and names of the designs. With a skein of colour thread as a teaching aid, the women can learn very fast.

When more careful research has been done, it is hoped a standardized textbook especially for these hilltribe people will be developed.

Having been exposed gently though directly and usefully to learning, it is expected that the hilltribers can be coaxed into the classroom of the development center or occasionally taught at their own houses. The Border Patrol Police teacher also invites the adults to sit in the classroom with their children, not only to see what is happening in the school but to get a pleasant taste of classroom environment. From this point it should not be too difficult a task to set up arrangements for a regular adult evening school. If the plan has not been discussed, the villagers could be led discreetly to suggest it themselves, assuming that they feel sufficiently at ease with the local Border Patrol Police.

In the classroom, a teacher follows up the technique originally employed to initiate interest in education on the part of the villagers. Flexibility through the frequent use of teaching aids would be demonstrated on the part of the Border Patrol Police teacher. Since some results are desired immediately, one concentrates on reading for meaning. Phonetic construction is a fine way to teach reading on a comprehensive and overall scale, but the entire process takes much too long. One of the greatest considerations that an instructor has to have in mind is the fact that he is dealing with a group of adults, mature in their own fashion, with as much learning and intelligence potential as any other congregation of individuals; yet overestimations of learning potential should not be made. A seeming retardation of progress is not usually caused by stupidity but by a clash of modes of thinking. Patience and understanding from the instructor are indispensable because the ways of the tribe are molded by tradition.

The classroom, as consistent with higher ideals of educational theory, is not just another place to drum out propaganda but a forum where ideas can be freely exchanged. The incessant use of propaganda, especially in the direction of adults, is a characteristic of the totalitarian state. Propaganda is desirable not only to impart basic knowledge to the adults of the hilltribers but also to introduce the idea that the tool of rational thought can be applied to adjustment in a world which has long since passed by.

The vast technological and industrial revolutions which have been shaking the earth, the force of the impact growing as time goes by, and the worldwide clash of ideology between different political ideas are far removed from the hills where the village tribemen live. The whole promise behind adult education for hilltribers is that one cannot wait generations for change to take place nor even the space of time it will take for present school children to grow into positions of responsibility in the village. The hilltriber cannot wait either.

One such tool of rational thought is that of critical thinking. Instead of feeding the villagers facts or propaganda, like the programming of a computer, discussion of learned material or pertinent subjects are encouraged.

Responses and opinions from the hilltribers are eagerly solicited by the instructor who indicates that he cares and is interested in what the hilltriber thinks. The villagers learn about the functions and purposes of their government as well as becoming enlightened about its faults. An objective discussion about the Thai system versus the one proposed by anti-government agitators could clear up fears and doubts relating to an allegiance to one or the other.

A Border Patrol Police instructor should not, in this situation, let his loyalty to the government cloud anything he says. The fact is that one cannot believe in any system because it is perfect since so far no systems have proved to be so. The Border Partol Police teachers are urged to point out why the Thai system is better off with a concept of allegiance to a government because it is one's own government. By their behavior and interest, the Border Patrol teachers, eventually infusing the villagers with the spirit to fight for their own land, have the ability to show that the Thai way is better.

By means of topical discussions, the idea of progress is given considerable light. Perhaps puzzles could be presented for the people to solve, ones which would demonstrate that there is more than one way to settle a problem. Rationally approached, each method of solution can be dissected and the easiest and most profitable method identified as a final solution.

This approach will help the villagers cope with difficulties intelligently. Villagers would know, for instance, when they find rats in one of their fields, that there are more ways to solve the problem than burning the entire field. The concept that there is more than one way of doing things should lead to a greater appreciation for and insight into the thought processes of other people, who are unlike them, and give them an inkling of the high potentialities of a human being. The people must learn that progress will not destroy their way of life, if they are prepared for it, but will broaden their lives and give them new proportions. The hilltribers need to be prepared for all life and to give it new proportions. The hilltribers need to be prepared for all kinds of adversities; they must know that rational analysis exploring all possibilities is a good tool. They also should know that to survive they must see further than one season. Plans can be made on a long-term basis for future benefit, and an attempt must be made to train those people to see education as a possible answer to their problems.

Conclusion

It is not our intention to use reading to "brainwash" the hilltriber into thinking like a modern Thai. We would, however, like to give them many things worth fighting for. It is very sad to see people starved and frightened. We cannot let them be swept away in an idealogical conflict when they know only distortions and shadows of the truth and when their patriotism can secure the safety of the whole country. Nor should we let them drift into the lowlands with the chance of doing only the lowest and most menial of tasks among their Thai brothers. Programs have been introduced which will allow the villager to realize that he can find a way to self-fulfillment.

HELEN HUUS

UNIVERSITY OF MISSOURI AT KANSAS CITY
KANSAS CITY, MISSOURI
UNITED STATES OF AMERICA

A Variety of Books

SOME AUTHORITIES include as literature only the creative works of imagination — ethereal, magical, fanciful, fictional works — and omit biography, science, and other writing labeled "nonfiction". But is literature confined solely to certain topics, or does the *treatment* of the topic make the difference?

The latter point of view recognizes the contribution that literary nonfiction makes to the total realm of literature, including literature for children as a part of that stream. And from the literature for children are drawn materials of various types or genre, on various topics and of varying levels of difficulty, to supplement the regular classroom materials in the basic school subjects. The supplementary books must meet the criteria of literary and artistic merit, each for its own type. In other words, a story must have a theme of significance, characters that are believably real (or believably fanciful), a plot that contains action and suspense, and a style that is appropriate, sincere, and vivid. Poetry must have an idea, a fresh way of seeing the ordinary, a rhythm and cadence befitting the subject, a natural (not forced) rhyme scheme, and a euphony of words that may sound like the full, round tones of an organ or the merry little notes of a street calliope. Nonfiction must be accurate in fact and feeling, precise and clear-cut in language, yet present bright images and apt figures of speech.

Such materials of many types contribute to the pupils' learning in several ways, only five of which will be discussed here.

1. *Books prepare the pupils for further studies*

In the early years of a child's life, the background provided by books is obvious for example, as children learn the traditional English Mother Goose rhymes like "Hey diddle, diddle", they become acquainted with the labels for domestic animals — cat, dog, cow — as depicted so cleverly by Randolph Caldecott (*1*) or Brian Wildsmith (*2*) in their illustrated editions. The wedding of Cock Robin, pictured so delicately by Barbara Cooney (*3*), shows a lovely bride in her traditional white dress and filmy veil, with the groom in proper formal attire and all the guests appropriately dressed for this festive occasion. Other rhymes extend vocabulary and concepts, too.

119

Children in other countries also have their traditional nursery rhymes that
are handed down from generation to generation orally until put into print and
thus preserved intact.

2. Books provide information that reinforces and supplements the textbooks

From the simple Japanese picture book, *Hippopotamus* by Eriko Kishida
(*4*), to others more complicated than this, stories about animals give information, even though in some the animals talk, as they do in Robert Lawson's
Rabbit Hill (*5*). Little Georgie, the hero, and the other animals are concerned
because a new family is moving into the house. However, all turns out well;
for they are "planting folk", and there is food enough for both the people and
the animals. A Finnish book entitled *Rabbits* by Kirsti Korpi (*6*) tells of their
habits and shows them in the cover picture well camouflaged for winter.

Poetry adds another dimension, yet can provide factual information like the
Norwegian poem about bats — the "flying mouse" that flits around from
house to house and goes to sleep upside down in trees (*7*) — or the unique
kiwi from New Zealand, who is very shy, in a poem by Ruth Coyle, "The
Kiwi" (*8*).

Older boys and girls are fascinated by the ingenuity and fortitude of three
unusual animal friends — a Siamese cat, an English bull terrior, and a Labora-
dor retriever — as they trudge over rough Canadian terrain to return to their
family. Their story is told by Sheila Burnford in her book entitled *The Incredible Journey* (*9*). Pupils are spellbound by the Newbery Award winner of
1949, *The King of the Wind* by Marguerite Henry (*10*), which tells about
the ancestors of the famous racehorse, Man-o'-War.

3. Books present a more detailed view than textbooks, for the latter so often must be compressed and inexpensively produced

Individual books on a single topic can present a larger close-up view, a
more detailed account than can a textbook. Books like the French *Tit . . . la
Mesange* by Anne-Marie Pajot (*11*), which shows wide-mouthed hungry birds
waiting to be fed, can do this, but it takes most of two pages to do so. Likewise, a familiar barnyard scene is pictured in a Swiss book on a larger scale
than would be possible in a textbook. Here the picture of a big, proud rooster,
resplendent in all his colorful glory, in the book *Knirps* by Max Bolliger (*12*),
covers a double page. Kauto, the friendly reindeer in the Norwegian book,
Kauto from Kautekeino by Jan-Magnus Bruheim (*13*), is pictured in his natural Arctic surroundings.

Photographs add reality, too, and Chendru's pet lion cub is shown in beautiful, colored reproductions in the Swedish book, *Chendru* by Astrid Sucksdorff (*14*).

4. Books give aesthetic experience through words and pictures

Knowingly or not, a reader absorbs and reacts to the format and illustration of books. *Do You See What I See?* by Helen Borten (*15*) helps him be aware of lines and shapes, like the triangle in the face of a fox or the beak of a bird. Books of art masterpieces, as reproduced in *The First Book of Art* by Pierre Belves and Francois Mathey (*16*) from France, help readers become familiar with these famous works. *Life Story* by Virginia Lee Burton (*17*) shows the evolution of life on earth through pictures that lead into and move along with the content of the text. Readers blow breezily along with the people in *The Wind* by Ib Spang Olsen (*18*) from Denmark, for his pictures sweep across the pages with great gusto. Poetry includes "Autumn Rain" from a Swedish collection by Eva Billow (*19*); and *The River* by Satoshi Kako (*20*) is a Japanese story of a stream flowing down to the sea.

5. Books put people into the content

Textbooks tend to be impersonal, but supplementary books can make other times seem contemporary and other places, familiar. *You Will Go to the Moon* by Mae and Ira Freeman (*21*) is a simple book, with less than 200 different words, and shows what is likely to happen on an expedition to explore the moon. *The Day We Saw the Sun Come Up* (*22*) describes the experience of two children who witness this glorious phenomena first-hand, and *Follow the Sunset* (*23*) tells of children around the world going to bed as the sun goes down and, thus, gives meaning to the concept of the earth's rotation.

It is in the realm of human relations that literature excels in extending and enhancing a reader's concept of the world and his neighbors and of himself. A topic such as "Everyday Life" could be introduced with the simple Japanese picture book *I Will Grow Up* by Seiichi Horiuchi (*24*); then *Everybody Has a Home* (*25*) from Iran could be added and put together with *Home* by Kamia Nair (*26*) from India, with illustrations showing Mother in her sari, Father in his fabric shop, and the children in Western dress. To extend the concept still further, *In My Mother's House* by Ann Nolan Clark (*27*) could be used, for it conveys the love and security felt by this American Indian child. Pelle, in Sweden (*28*), is just as proud of his new suit as the Iranian child is of his new red coat in a book of that title (*29*).

Other books describe everyday activities of children, in *Ali Goes to the Zoo* (*30*) from Turkey and in *Katherine* by Elisabeth MacIntyre (*31*) from Australia, where the heroine takes good care of her horse. *David, Boy of the High Country* by Georg Kohlap (*32*) tells of a boy in New Zealand playing and reading while his compatriot, a little Maori boy, attends school in *Hey, Boy!* (*33*).

Children learn to meet and face problems in books. In America, *The Jazz*

Man by Mary Hays Weik (*34*) tells how he moves into the empty apartment across the street in Harlem from little crippled Zeke and how he relieves Zeke's loneliness and plays the tiredness out of the mother's feet. In Maine, little Sal loses her tooth but gets her wish of an ice cream cone, anyway, as told in *One Morning in Maine* (*35*), which is written and illustrated by Sal's father, Robert McCloskey. The story of Sam (short for "Samantha"), Bangs, her cat, and Moonshine, which is what her father calls the stories she tells that are not true, is pictured and told by Evaline Ness (*36*), and Sam learns that telling falsehoods does not pay. Robert McCloskey, whose stories are sometimes reminiscent of his boyhood in a small town, in his book *Homer Price* (*37*) describes some of the escapades typical of such boys, including the well-known episode of the doughnut machine that will not stop.

Ethical issues are also treated in books. Little Wanda is teased by the children because she says she has a hundred dresses all lined up in her closet at home; then the children find out these are her drawings (*38*). Crow Boy, who walks to school each morning alone and stays aloof from the group, is discovered by an understanding teacher to be able to imitate the various calls of the crows. His story is told and pictured sympathetically in *Crow Boy* by Taro Yashima (*39*). Hans Christian Andersen's story of *The Ugly Duckling* (40) teaches another lesson, as does *Two is a Team* by Lorraine and Jerrold Beim (*41*), which shows two little boys, one white and the other Negro, the advantages of working together.

Well-written biographies of famous men and women add historical fact and portray characters with personality: Augustus Caesar, Queen Elizabeth I, and Napoleon; Pasteur, Galileo, and Newton; or Captain Cook, Henry Hudson, and George Washington. Biographies have been written about many such famous figures in history.

Stories of frontier life in the American Midwest are vividly told in "The Little House" books by Laura Ingalls Wilder (*42*) and in *Caddie Woodlawn* by Carol Ryrie Brink (*43*). The nineteenth century is made believable by *Little Women* (*44*), *Hans Brinker* (*45*), and the Danish *Peter's Christmas* (*46*) and *Flight to America* (*47*).

Perhaps the greatest contribution that supplementary books can make is to give the reader the feeling that he is "there". Such books as Sasek's *This is —* series, represented by *This is Hong Kong* (*48*), pictures the streets, the people, and the buildings as they are and as they give distinction to each locale. The classic *The Australia Book* (*49*) and *A Picture History of Australia* (*50*) combine history and geography, and a book of poems entitled *One Sunday Morning Early* by Irene Gough (*51*) catches the Australian flavor well, as the introductory selection, entitled "Treasure", exemplifies.

Exciting adventures, either folk tales or modern stories, extend horizons for readers by describing customs and taboos and values of other societies. *Call it*

Courage, a Polynesian legend told by Armstrong Sperry (52), relates how Mafatu found his courage; *Daughter of the Mountains* by Louise Rankin (53) describes Nepalese Momo's trek over the mountains to Calcutta to find her stolen red-gold llhasa terrior, Pempa; and *The Good Master* by Kate Seredy (54) traces the gentling of the spirited Hungarian tomboy Kate by her uncle, "the good master". Add to this last book, the majestic story of the Hungarian people as they journey to their promised land, which is told and illustrated by the same author-artist in *The White Stag* (55), for the myths of these people are part of their heritage, just like the myths of Greece and Rome or the giants and trolls of Norway. These latter are pictured so realistically by the noted artist Thor Kittelsen, (56), for he had, by his own admission, *seen* one, though contemporary artist Marcia Brown, a non-Norwegian, manages also to capture their spirit in her *Three Billy Goats Gruff* (57).

Unless the pictures and stories of other lands are authentic, young readers can acquire much misinformation. Compare, for example, the Paris of *Madeline* by Ludwig Bemelmans (58) with photographs of the Eiffel Tower, the Opera, and Notre Dame, and notice the similarity of mood and detail.

These few examples show several ways by which supplementary books of different types — fiction, poetry, folklore, and biography — provide readiness, reinforcement, breadth, and depth to science and the social studies and portray in historical and international perspective the ingenuity of man as he has approached his problems through time and learned how to cope with his surroundings and his neighbors. In the reading, a reader can play many roles in many eras; he can experience a range of emotions; and he can become sensitive to the recurring problems of mankind. But he can also *enjoy* books, for as Lillian Smith (59) has said so well:

> ... there *is* magic in the writing of ... (children's) books ... The essence from which it is distilled can best be discovered in those books which generations of children have taken to their hearts and have kept alive, books which seem to have an immortality that adult books, so soon superseded by the latest best-seller, seldom attain.

It is such books that supplement today's teaching and that help pupils realize the common humanity of man the world over.

BIBLIOGRAPHY

1. Randolph Caldecott. *The Hey Diddle Diddle Picture Book.* London: Warne, 1879.
2. *Brian Wildsmith's Mother Goose.* New York: Watts, 1964.
3. Barbara Cooney. *The Courtship, Merry Marriage, and Feast of Cock Robin and Jenny Wren, to Which is Added the Doleful Death of Cock Robin.* New York: Scribner, 1965.
4. Eriko Kishida. *Hippopotamus.* Kanda-Tokyo: Fukuinkan-Shoten, 1962.
5. Robert Lawson. *Rabbit Hill.* New York: Viking, 1944.

6. Kirsti Korpi. *Janis.* Helsinki: Otava, 1965.
7. Inger Hagerup. *Så Rart.* Oslo: Aschehoug, 1950.
8. Dorothy Laycock and Ruth Coyle. *Tell Me About New Zealand: Poems for Children.* Auckland: Pelorus, n.d.
9. Scheila Burford. *The Incredible Journey.* Boston: Little, 1961.
10. Marguerite Henry. *The King of the Wind.* Chicago: Rand, 1948.
11. Anne-Marie Pajot. *Tit ... la Mesange.* Paris: Hatier, 1965.
12. Max Bolliger. *Knirps.* Winterthur: Comenius, 1961.
13. Jan-Magnus Bruheim. *Reinsbukken Kauto fra Kautokeino.* Oslo: Noreg, 1966.
14. Astrid Sucksdorff. *Chendru får en Tiger.* Stockholm: Bonniers, n.d.
15. Helen Borten. *Do You See What I See?* New York: Abelard, 1959.
16. Pierre Belves and Francois Mathey. *Premier Livre D'Art.* Paris: Gautier—Languereau, 1965.
17. Virginia Lee Burton. *Life Story.* Boston: Houghton, 1962.
18. Ib Spang Olsen. *Blaesten.* Copenhagen: Gyldendal, 1963.
19. Eva Billow. *Jag Tycker Mest om Plättar.* Stockholm: Nordisk Rotogravyr, n.d.
20. Satoshi Kako. *The River.* Kanda-Tokyo: Fukuinkan-Shoten, 1962.
21. Mae and Ira Freeman. *You Will Go to the Moon.* New York: Random, 1959.
22. Alice E. Goudey. *The Day We Saw the Sun Come Up.* New York: Scribner, 1961.
23. Herman and Nina Schneider. *Follow the Sunset.* New York: Doubleday, 1952.
24. Seiichi Horiuchi. *I Will Grow Up!* Kanda-Tokyo: Fukuinkan-Shoten, 1964.
25. Lily Ayman. *Everybody Has a Home.* Teheran: Bongah-e Tarjomeh va Nashr-e Ketab, n.d.
26. Kamia Nair. *Home.* New Delhi: Children's Book Trust, 1965.
27. Ann Nolan Clark. *In My Mother's House.* New York: Viking, 1941.
28. Elsa Beskow. *Pelles Nya Kläder.* Stockholm: Bonniers, n.d.
29. Lily Ayman. *The Red Coat.* Teheran: Bongah-e Tarjomeh va Nashr-e Ketab, n.d.
30. *Ali Hayvanlar Bahçesinde.* Ankara: Yayim, 1963.
31. Elisabeth MacIntyre. *Katherine. Sydney:* Angus & Robertson, 1963.
32. Georg Kohlap. *David, Boy of the High Country.* London: Collins, 1965.
33. Jane and Bernie Hill. *Hey Boy!* Christchurch: Whitcombe and Tombs, 1962.
34. Mary Hays Weik. *The Jazz Man.* New York: Atheneum, 1967.　　..
35. Robert McCloskey. *One Morning in Maine.* New York: Viking, 1952.
36. Evaline Ness. *Sam, Bangs & Moonshine.* New York: Holt, 1966.
37. Robert McCloskey. *Homer Price.* New York: Viking, 1943.
38. Eleanor Estes. *The Hundred Dresses.* New York: Harcourt, 1944.
39. Taro Yashima. *Crow Boy.* New York: Viking, 1955.
40. Hans Christian Andersen. *Den Grimme Aelling.* Copenhagen: Gyldendal, 1963.
41. Lorraine and Jerrold Beim: *Two is a Team.* New York: Harcourt, 1945.
42. Laura Ingalls Wilder. *The Little House in the Big Woods.* New York: Harper, 1932, 1953.
43. Carol Ryrie Brink. *Caddie Woodlawn.* New York: Macmillan, 1935.
44. Louisa May Alcott. *Little Women.* Boston: Little, 1867.
45. Mary Mapes Dodge. *Hans Brinker: or the Silver Skates.* New York: Scribner, 1915.
46. J. Krohn. *Peters Jul.* Copenhagen: Gyldendal, 1965.
47. Christian Winther. *Flugeten til Amerika.* Copenhagen: Gyldendal, 1966.
48. M. Sasek. *This is Hong Kong.* New York: Macmillan, 1965.
49. Eve Pownall. *The Australia Book.* Sydney: John Sands, n.d.
50. R. M. Crawford. *A Picture History of Australia.* London: Oxford, 1961.
51. Irene Gough. *One Sunday Morning Early.* Sydney: Ure Smith, 1963.
52. Armstrong Sperry. *Call It Courage.* New York: Macmillan, 1940.
53. Louise Rankin. *Daughter of the Mountains.* New York: Viking, 1948.
54. Kate Seredy. *The Good Master.* New York: Viking, 1935.
55. Kate Seredy. *The White Stag.* New York: Viking, 1937.
56. P. Chr. Asbjørnsen. *Illustrerede Eventyr.* Oslo: Gyldendal, 1906.
57. P. C. Asbjornsen and J. E. Moe. *The Three Billy Goats Gruff.* New York: Harcourt, 1957.
58. Ludwig Bemelmans. *Madeline.* New York: Viking, 1939.
59. Lillian Smith. *The Unreluctant Years.* New York: Viking, 1967, p. 11.

RICHARD BAMBERGER

FUHRMANNSGASSE 18 A
1080 VIENNA 8
AUSTRIA

The Joy of Reading

THE WRITER'S CONTRIBUTION to this international forum is primarily based on the central European cultural sphere, in particular the German and Slavonic speaking areas and also, to a certain extent, France. Some ideas will, therefore, seem quite self-evident to American experts; other ideas may not raise the necessary responses to Americans at all.

The main drawbacks of the school reading matter of the past have been their complete isolation, their lack of relevance to the children's lives, and their complete disregard of private reading. As early as 1903 the German writer Heinrich Hart drew the following conclusion during the art education conference in Weimar, "More important than all school reading is the fact that the teacher should win a lasting influence on a child's private reading".

"Supplementary reading" in the context of this paper is not only reading matter covered in school in addition to prescribed texts. Supplementary reading includes nonfiction read for the various school subjects and primarily that reading usually called "private reading", i. e., the entire reading matter of young people. Supplementary reading is, in fact, all the reading matter that can open up the entire field of literature leading to an involvement with literature and to its use in self-education.

The final aim of this paper is to demolish the rift between school reading and private reading, an aim which means that school materials should also be read privately and, conversely, private reading matter should also be read in school. The more immediate task, however, is to establish bridges between school and private reading and to influence the entire reading habits of children, so that positive literature replaces the negative. Each reader should receive what he wants and needs, according to his interests and potential.

If one is to fulfill this aim of giving the reader what he needs and wants, in the light of his potential development, one must first know the reader. By this statement is not meant one should study him as a psychological type, evaluating his reading interests, his reading patterns, and his particular reading stimuli. Untill now it has been considered merely a question of finding the right book for the right child at the right moment. This axiom fascinates the librarians above all.

However, no one appears to have thought of asking whether that child could read a book or whether he had developed the necessary reading skill and comprehension to be able to cope with books, not only the books for beginning readers but also books suitable for later stages. A number of studies on this problem were conducted during the past few years in Austria; and the concept of "book readiness" was examined mainly from the point of view of reading level attainment. These investigations brought the following paradox to light.

Why some Children do not Read

Many children read no books because they cannot read, and they cannot read because they read no books. To explain, in a large number of schools an average of 40 percent of the children could not read well enough to justify the hope that they might really enjoy reading a book. The inquiry, by the way, covered about 30,000 children and concentrated on their skill in silent reading. It became obvious that these children would hardly ever reach for a book on their own initiative. However, there were also many schools that showed an entirely different pattern: by the second school year 70 to 80 percent were fond of reading books. In the third and fourth years this percentage rose to even 80 to 90 percent.

Investigations showed that reading instruction in the average classes was based on primers and readers by the old method of oral reading. In the exceptional classes, the readers introduced supplementary reading matter which awakened a joy in reading from the very beginning. Two prerequisites were always present here: 1) interested, well-informed, and alert teachers who were enthusiastic readers themselves and 2) abundant materials. The teachers raised eager anticipation through storytelling and reading to the class and provided easy picture books and children's books which the children could read by themselves to experience the joy of achievement. The books were provided by the Austrian Children's Book Club.

The children's approach to the books was made easier by the teachers' telling a section of the book, then reading to the children, and finally letting them read on. No distinction existed between school and private reading. After reading was started in school, it was continued at home. These tests of "book readiness" have no scientific pretensions. The tests are not meant as research but rather for practical application in school. They are intended as an "alarm signal" and as a challenge to the teacher.

The procedure is briefly as follows: little 32-page booklets are distributed for silent reading; after half an hour or an hour the number of pages (or words) read by the children is counted; next to reading speed, perseverence is a primary sign of "book readiness"; subsequently, comprehension of content and understanding of the essence of the text are checked.

Seen purely from the point of view of reading technique, the first obvious result was that second grade pupils who read approximately 3,000 words in thirty minutes will usually read a book with pleasure. Children who read fewer pages need help. In the fourth year of school, children who cannot read approximately 4,500 words in thirty minutes can be considered as backward readers. These tests of book readiness are the basis for dividing each school class into three main groups: the best group, the group at grade level, and the group needing special attention. The primary task of reading education is to give all three groups suitable incentives.

Supplementary Reading

Among the many opportunities open to the teacher, primary concern is with supplementary reading. This category can be considered from two points of view: selection, (i. e. to what kind of literature is one to guide children?) and the methods of guidance towards literature. Selection usually takes into consideration the work units of school, and the teacher looks for appropriate reading matter. This phase is important as a vehicle of education, as a working tool. In literary education, however, it can be a disadvantage, for reading is then considered primarily as an agent for the transmission of knowledge.

One should, however, consider this type of reading as an end in itself. The selection of reading matter should put less stress on educational value than on the aesthetic pleasure. Literary value takes first place, then follows the psychological point of view, the adjustment to the young reader, and finally the educational and instructive significance. More important than the selection is guidance towards such reading. Observance of the ancient pedagogic precepts "from the easy to the more difficult" is decisive — meaning not so much the matter of *easy* or *more difficult* literature as *easing* the reception of such literature, smoothing the paths to books. Schools of the old type tried to meet the difficulties of a text through explaining difficult words, concepts, and psychological background. This procedure did not make reading easier, only much more boring.

One now knows that children primarily love subject matter, plot, and events. To win a child for a book, lead him into the subject matter, into the plot — indeed, even lure him into it. How is that possible? If, beside the stocks of school or class library, where each book is usually available in one copy only, important — i. e. particularly valuable, exciting, and suitable — books are made available in the same number as there are pupils (or books can be borrowed from a central institution) so that each pupil can read the same book not only in school but primarily at home. The teacher or some pupils introduce the book by telling a section of the story and reading a section to the class. Then the pupils read on in school and at home.

This method seems to contradict the premise: the right book for the right child at the right moment. This conclusion is partly correct. However, there are a few books which are so strong that they appeal to almost all children. If one succeeds by this method in educating children to become good readers, they will also find the way to selecting their books individually. Therefore, one of the main tasks of reading education is to provide each group with the right supplementary reading matter in addition to the official school readers.

In Europe, and in particular in the German-speaking area, there is great respect for the original versions of books. Simplified versions, for instance, are unknown; and there is certainly no need for simplified editions for children who read well and eagerly. For backward readers, however, the question arises "What is better, having simple texts written by someone who is not capable of creating atmospheres or convincing characters? or simplifying high quality books for these readers?" In a spirit of service to the readers and to the education of future readers of good books, this writer advocates responsible editing of simplified versions for supplementary reading.

Nonfiction

Learning to read through books is, therefore, complemented by learning to work with books. Here again the right path leads from the easy to the more difficult and means adaptation to the abilities and the potentialities of individual pupils or groups of pupils.

It used to be considered sufficient to point out the treasures waiting in the library to young people in their last, difficult years of school. One has since realized that habits must be established early if one wants to prepare students for life. Work with books must start in the earliest years of primary school. The habit of looking things up in encyclopedias and following up an interesting topic by referring to books suitable for the particular reading level ought to become firmly established. This suggestion may seem self-evident, but there are still far too many schoolrooms without even the most essential reference works. It is most important to introduce from the very beginning supplementary reading that is both easy and gripping, in addition to the textbooks for the various subjects.

In England and America there are numerous series like *The Story of Food, The Story of Clothing,* of housing, of transport, coal, water, and the like. Others must study these series thoroughly and to encourage publishers to produce books to fulfill that need for their respective countries. At present the usual policy is to produce translations because of the advantage of using the available pictorial material. However, children are not very fond of these books because all too frequently they contain foreign concepts and because points of reference to the familiar environment are lacking. One is aware of the fact that publishers will produce large-scale projects only if the prospects of success are good. Teachers and librarians, therefore, must make use of the few possibilities available and systematically lead the children to books which correspond to their mental growth.

In Central Europe there is massive opposition to books introducing children to foreign countries too early. The native land should be given prominence. This point of view certainly has some validity. However, the world now confronts the child at a very early age through television, films, periodicals, even in the windows of any large department store. One must make this confrontation with the encroaching world easier for the child and is, therefore, justified in offering the child first books on the world at large as well as books on his own country, even during the first reading stages.

Concluding Statement

The English-speaking area has been able to amass much experience on the question of supplementary reading not only with regard to book production but also in regard to the use of books. Others can learn from this experience but must not adopt it blindly. The central problem is fusion of tradition and of new elements. If one knows the destination well, a way will be found.

The first aim is not merely to teach reading but to educate readers. He who has been taught to read has mastered a skill; he who has become a reader is a different person. In the confrontation with literature he has become conscious of his abilities and personality and has developed his own indivudual tastes. This development of character and cultivation of taste have put him in a position to make discriminating use of mass media. The second aim is a systematic introduction to the world of books as a means of helping the individual adapt to an ever-changing world as a means of continuous information and further education and also as an aid to developing a personal attitude toward life. These tasks, the wakening of the personality and the comprehension of the world, present the most intrinsic cultural challenges of the times. Books have a most essential contribution to make in this task.

TEACHER EDUCATION

HELEN M. ROBINSON

THE UNIVERSITY OF CHICAGO
CHICAGO, ILLINOIS
UNITED STATES OF AMERICA

Preparation of Reading Specialists in the U.S.A.

CLASSROOM TEACHERS in the U.S.A. have varying amounts of preparation for teaching reading. Many have taken a course in language arts which includes listening, speaking, reading, and writing. Others have taken one or more courses in teaching reading, and a few have been carefully observed in their practice teaching by reading instructors. In some instances, teachers trained for secondary schools have been assigned to the early grades. Moreover, a number of teachers from earlier years have returned to teaching in order to meet the demands of the burgeoning elementary school population. Thus, the differences in preparation of classroom teachers have created a demand for specialists to help meet the needs of a diverse population of school children.

Types of Specialists

Various titles are used for reading specialists, many of whom perform similar functions. A systematic survey by Dever (3), published in 1956, revealed that different titles were applied to those who worked in schools, clinics, and in teacher preparation. In her concluding chapter, Dever attributed the confusion, first, to the fact that this was a relatively new field in which at least one-fifth were "pioneers" without any preparation for their positions. Second, she concluded that positions were created hurriedly and that the limited number of trained specialists resulted in promotion of able classroom teachers who attempted to develop the necessary competencies after assuming their positions.

In the past decade, various writers have surveyed and delineated the major responsibilities of specialists who are given particular titles (7). Unfortunately there is some disagreement among writers. Likewise, there are marked differences among the programs designed to prepare specialists who bear the same titles. Therefore, a brief resume will be given of the responsibilities assigned to specialists bearing certain titles before a description of their preparation is presented.

The *remedial reading teacher* usually serves one or more schools, and his

133

major function is to help pupils who are retarded in reading. He may teach small groups of children or, occasionally, individuals. In some instances the remedial teacher also helps classroom teachers in meeting the needs of pupils, primarily to correct minor difficulties and to prevent the development of reading retardation.

The *reading clinician* is usually a member of the staff of a reading clinic, either in a school system or at a college or university. There are some private reading clinics in the U. S. A., varying considerably in the types of preparation of staff members. Some reading clinicians serve as members of teams in units, such as language centers, hospitals, and the like.

The reading clinician should be skilled in individual diagnosis and in offering remedial instruction to severely retarded readers. Because of the gravity of the problems presented by reading clinic clients, the clinician must be conversant with specialists in allied fields whose services may be needed to correct other factors which interfere with learning.

Reading clinics connected with colleges and universities usually provide demonstration and practicum experience for teachers in reading. Clinics operated by school systems often prepare remedial reading teachers by offering in-service training. In some school systems, teachers are assigned to clinics for a semester to develop competence in remedial instruction.

The *reading consultant,* a member of the staff of one or more schools, has the primary responsibility of assisting the total school staff continuously in the improvement of reading instruction. In their handbook for the reading consultant, Robinson and Rauch (6) included the following major roles: resource person, advisor, in-service leader, investigator, diagnostician, instructor, and evaluator. In a small school system, the consultant may serve both elementary and secondary schools. In a larger system, a consultant may serve at either or all levels.

The *reading coordinator* may be the administrator responsible for a number of consultants in the school system. In other schools, the *reading supervisor* or the *language arts supervisor* has this responsibility. The supervisor is usually responsible for rating teachers, handling budgets, and performing other administrative duties.

College teachers of reading are those who prepare classroom teachers and other reading specialists described in the previous sections. In addition to offering courses, many college reading teachers supervise their students during the apprentice-teaching period and offer a wide range of services to school personnel in their local and state areas. Most of them write articles or books, evaluate instructional materials, and carry on some types of action or experimental research.

Researchers in reading are usually university professors who teach graduate courses, supervise masters' and doctoral students, and have some time allotted to their own research. In recent years, a few persons are devoting full-time to reading research, usually in centers sponsored by the U. S. government.

To summarize, a number of specialists in reading have been needed in the U. S. A. in recent years. Many "specialists" have been inadequately prepared for their responsibilities. Only in recent years have selected colleges and universities addressed themselves to the problem of preparing specialists rather than generalists.

Sources of Information

In order to present a fairly representative description of programs for reading specialists, two sources were used. First, an extensive survey of graduate programs was made by Wilson (8) who published a brief report from approximately 175 colleges and universities in 45 states in the U. S. A. and three provinces in Canada. However, no details of the programs were given to assist in the descriptions planned for this paper.

Second, a questionnaire was devised and circulated by the writer, beginning in November 1967. The first mailing was to universities known to be engaged in preparing some types of reading specialists. Moreover, each respondent was asked to name other colleges and universities to which questionnaires were sent subsequently. In all, 133 questionnaires were mailed, and 94 replies were received from 23 states. Of those who replied, 84 offered special reading programs while ten did not. Many of the respondents included program descriptions which were tabulated and summarized.

All graduate programs included a master's degree, with various designations. Some degrees are offered in reading; others, in language arts or in elementary or secondary education with a major in reading. A few master of science in teaching degrees are offered, some with field experience in schools. At the University of Chicago, a master of science in teaching degree is planned especially for reading consultants. In addition to four quarters devoted to academic courses, the prospective consultants spend a year as interns.

Eight respondents have a sixth-year program, or a year beyond the master's degree. Some grant a special certificate in reading while others give a certificate of advanced study. The programs differ in that a variety of types of specialists are being prepared in different ways.

The Ed. D. is given by 23 universities and the Ph. D., by 22, some of which offer both degrees. Generally the latter have a greater emphasis on research although there is considerable communality in the programs for the degrees. No mention was made of post-doctoral training elsewhere, although the University of Chicago has had a post-doctoral research associate each year since 1961.

Many respondents stated that their programs were designed to meet their respective state certification requirements and/or the minimum requirements recommended by the International Reading Association.

Standards for Specialists

Prior to 1960 only a few surveys of the duties of specialists were available to guide colleges and universities in planning their programs. Furthermore, state departments of education did not certify professional reading specialists. As a result, many programs were extremely limited; often graduates were unable to meet the demands of the responsibilities imposed on them by schools and colleges. In 1961 the International Reading Association prepared and approved minimum standards which were published. Revised standards (5) were published in 1965; a standing committee continues to reevaluate these minimum standards and has undertaken the task of differentiating standards for various positions. At the time this paper was written, the Minimum Standards for Classroom Teachers (4) was the only other printed publication.

The minimum standards for specialists are designed especially for those who work primarily with developmental and remedial reading in schools. The pamphlet states that reading consultants, supervisors, directors, and clinicians need further training; suggestions for the kinds of training are now being considered.

The brochure describing minimum standards for specialists of reading states that three years of successful classroom or clinical experience should be a prerequisite to admission. The specialist should have a master's degree or the equivalent in credits. A minimum of three courses in reading include 1) foundations or survey of reading; 2) diagnosis and correction of reading disabilities; and 3) clinical or laboratory practicum in reading which provides supervised practice in diagnosis and remedial instruction. A second part of the program offers choices among courses in measurement and evaluation psychology, literature for children and adolescents, linguistics and language development, and/or curriculum and supervision.

The minimum standards have been the essential guide to the eleven states in the U. S. A. that now license some types of reading specialists. Moreover, other states are considering special certification at present.

Of the 175 programs listed by Wilson, only twelve reported that theirs did not meet these minimum standards. More than half of the 86 who answered the questionnaire for the present paper had expectations well beyond the minimum standards, and 46 replied that plans were underway to extend their present programs. Several types of additions were suggested but three predominated: 1) a broader academic range, such as adding secondary and college levels to the present program for elementary specialists; 2) supervised practice in clinics or schools; and 3) research orientation such as critical reading of research, application of research findings, and design of action and/or experimental research. There was a minor but growing trend toward understanding and working cooperatively with related disciplines, such as linguistics, neurology, psychiatry, and sociology.

Programs for Preparing Specialists

Specific types of preparation appear to have a number of common elements, as well as some unique requirements or expectations of the different colleges and universities. Some typical and a few deviatory programs will be described for each specialty.

The *remedial reading teacher* is usually expected to have been a successful classroom teacher prior to entering the program. The majority of programs for special training in this area include some courses or understanding of history, philosophy, psychology, and/or sociology of education.

A course entitled foundations or survey of reading is designed to acquaint the graduate student with developmental reading plans so that he will know the sequence of skills developed at different grade levels and understand how pupils acquire reading skills and abilities. This type of understanding is essential in order to assess the amount and character of retardation exhibited by individual pupils who fall behind the regular developmental program and become retarded readers.

Most respondents mentioned one or two courses dealing with diagnosis and correction of reading difficulties. Some survey the causes of reading retardation. Diagnosis, in all descriptions, gives intensive attention to familiarity with informal and standardized survey tests and to some diagnostic reading tests. Graduate students are expected to become competent in administering and interpreting the scores. Observations of diagnoses appear to make the courses more meaningful. Some courses provide acquaintance with screening tests to identify pupils who should be referred to refractionists or psychologists for further diagnoses in their special areas.

The corrective aspects include the study of methods of remedial instruction and familiarity with commercial instructional materials. A plethora of books, workbooks, games, machines, and tradebooks is available. Recently some programmed instructional materials have been published. Criteria for selecting and methods for adapting materials to the needs of small groups and to individuals within groups are essential parts of the courses. Methods for evaluating progress are included, and attention is usually given to the performance of pupils in their own classroom groups. Observations of skilled remedial teachers may be a part of the program.

A third type of course designated as practium is usually a part of the preparation provided. Graduate students may diagnose and teach small groups of children under the supervision of a master remedial teacher.

The *reading clinician* is expected to acquire the knowledge and competencies of the remedial reading teacher. In addition, he learns the individual case-study techniques which permit greater breadth, depth, and accuracy of diagnosis than are possible in group sessions.

Interview techniques are learned to acquire adequate case histories. In addition, emphasis is given to individual testing of some or all of the following: intelligence, language development, aptitudes requisite to modes of learning to recognize words, identification of deficits in comprehension skills, and problems of adequacy of rate of reading.

Increased familiarity with factors that inhibit learning to read and with the research dealing with these factors may be considered essential. Instruction is usually given in administering and interpreting tests to identify children or youth with visual, neurological, hearing, and/or emotional difficulties. Acquaintance is provided with referral sources among allied professions. Ways to write effective reports to parents, teachers, and related professional groups may be scrutinized.

Special attention is given to individually adapted methods of instruction and to diagnostic teaching. Teacher-made materials of special value to severely retarded readers are illustrated. Prospective clinicians also learn to teach the techniques they use to others and are especially prepared to write interpretive reports to teachers and parents.

Whenever reading clinics are available, practice in both diagnosis and instruction under careful supervision is expected. In a few instances an internship provides wider experiences with many types of cases and contacts with related professional groups.

Preparation for the *reading consultant* includes the understandings and competencies to teach reading at elementary and secondary levels, in regular classrooms, and to retarded readers. Prospective consultants need to know the means for assessing the reading progress of pupils and the ability to interpret test scores to administrators, teachers, and parents. They should become familiar with current curriculums in reading, language arts, and related content areas. Techniques for revising old curriculums and developing new ones are learned. Psychological understandings of learning, of dealing with groups to prepare for inservice training of teachers, and of dealing effectively with individual teachers are considered important.

Frequently principles are learned for evaluating and applying research. With the advent of government grants, attention has been given to preparing proposals to secure funds for improving practices and for action-research to evaluate innovations.

A few universities offer field experiences in making surveys, in planning programs, and in the like. For eight years the University of Chicago has required a year of internship; one quarter is spent in the reading clinic; a second quarter is in a public elementary school under the supervision of a competent reading consultant; a third quarter is spent at the secondary level, with a consultant, working with content-area teachers to help them improve the reading of their students in these areas. Most programs for consultants are included in masters' degrees or require a year beyond the masters' degree.

The *reading coordinator* is expected to have all of the understandings and competencies of the consultant plus training in administration and supervision. Very few programs are designed to prepare coordinators, probably because only large schools systems have such positions available.

College teachers of reading are expected to have obtained the Ed. D. or Ph. D. degrees. Unfortunately, an insufficient number of these persons is available so that many courses for the preparation of classroom teachers are offered by generalists in elementary education, in language arts, or even in other areas, such as curriculum. Reluctantly, some colleges are appointing methods teachers with masters' degrees or certificates of advanced study. Reading consultants may be employed to give courses at nearby colleges.

The respondents to the writer's questionnaire who described their programs for college teachers generally offered advanced degrees in education or psychology with a major or special field of reading. The number of courses in reading per se varies from four to twenty-two. Related areas include general curriculum, psychology, linguistics, literature for children and youth, statistics, research design, and various assistantships. The methods-teaching assistant is mentioned by several, but no information is provided about the kinds of direction offered to these young people. Austin (1) has made a strong plea for improving the quality of preparation of college instructors of reading courses.

At the University of Chicago an experimental course has been given for advanced doctoral candidates specializing in reading to help them plan and teach a reading methods course. Rather than emulate their own instructors as is often the practice, they set goals described in behavioral terms for a unique group of students, planned the sequence of learnings to achieve these goals, developed the topics and procedures sequentially, and determined valuation procedures. Later in the academic year, they gave two sections of the course; the second section was improved on the basis of group evaluation of the first.

Reading researchers usually hold the doctoral degree and have been prepared in departments of psychology, linguistics, or education. Until recently, most researchers have had degrees in education. In a survey of reading researchers, Barton and Wilder (2) pointed out the deficits in preparation prior to 1964 and especially to the low values placed on reading research both by producers and consumers. Since that time, research training grants have been made available, and many universities have taken steps to strengthen their programs. Moreover, interaction with allied disciplines has been helpful in stimulating more rigorous research training. The availability of computers has led to different research designs. Graduate students are sometimes expected to demonstrate research competence prior to beginning their dissertations. Research internships, in which doctoral candidates work as part of a team headed by a major researcher, are becoming more prevalent.

The quality of research produced suggests that the preparation of reading researchers has been the least effective of the programs for reading specialists. Continuous efforts are being made to improve this program in the U. S. A. Furthermore, most of the other programs are under continuous scrutiny, and plans are being made in a number of colleges and universities for improvement.

Concluding Statement

As the need for various types of reading specialists has increased, the colleges and universities have responded by planning various programs to prepare the specialists. Depending upon the functions which the specialists are expected to serve, preparation varies from a few courses to the program for the doctorate. Not nearly enough specialists are being prepared; consequently, untrained people are being pressed into positions for which they are not prepared. Inservice training is being provided in summer sessions and during the academic year to help supply the quantity and quality of leadership needed to improve reading instruction and basic research in reading throughout the United States.

REFERENCES

1. Austin, Mary C. "Professional Training of Reading Personnel", in Helen M. Robinson (Ed.), *Innovation and Change in Reading Instruction,* 67th Yearbook of the National Society for the Study of Education, Part 2. Chicago: University of Chicago Press, 1968.
2. Barton, Allen H., and David E. Wilder. "Research and Practice in the Teaching of Reading: A Progress Report", in Matthew B. Miles (Ed), *Innovation in Education.* New York: Bureau of Publications, Teachers College, Columbia University, 1964.
3. Dever, Kathryn Imogene. *Positions in the Field of Reading.* New York: Bureau of Publications, Teachers College, Columbia University, 1956.
4. Professional Standards and Ethics Committee, International Reading Association. *Minimum Standards for Professional Preparation in Reading for Classroom Teachers,* Newark, Delaware, 1965.
5. Professional Standards and Ethics Committee, International Reading Association. *Minimum Standards for Professional Training of Reading Specialists,* Newark, Delaware, 1965.
6. Robinson, H. Alan, and Sidney J. Rauch. *Guiding the Reading Program.* Chicago: Science Research Associates, 1965.
7. Robinson, Helen M. "The Role of Special Services in the Reading Program", in J. Allen Figurel (Ed.), *New Frontiers in Reading.* New York: Scholastic Magazines, 1960, 160—164.
8. Wilson, Robert M. "Colleges and Universities Offering Programs in Reading", *Journal of the Reading Specialist,* 7 (December 1967), 66—87.

Dina Feitelson

THE HEBREW UNIVERSITY
JERUSALEM, ISRAEL

Training Teachers of Disadvantaged Children

Cultural Diversity

THE TERMS culturally deprived or culturally disadvantaged have lately become the object of criticism on the American educational scene (5, 6, 7). Israel shares essentially the same kind of problems; yet the terminology which grew up around them, as well as the ways developed to deal with these problems, is somewhat different. While the United States has often been referred to as a "melting pot", Israel is sometimes called a "pressure cooker". In the past twenty years the Jewish population in Israel multiplied fourfold. The number of pupils in the school system has increased correspondingly. The parents of these pupils come from many different countries, but especially from the underdeveloped countries of the Near East and North Africa. Today, 60 percent of each year's first graders in the Jewish school system is of Middle-Eastern or North African parentage.

Child-rearing patterns in these communities differ basically from child-rearing patterns in so called western societies. And as originally the educational system in Israel was organized along western lines, these children lack many of the skills, aptitudes, and attitudes which are prerequisites for coping successfully with a western-type educational system.

In short, cultural diversity on the part of the society, combined with an educational framework which is geared solely to the needs, aspirations, and human qualities of only one of the subcultures represented in the society, produces school failure in the other segments.

As already mentioned, the extremely high proportion of children from a non-western cultural background in Israeli society makes the problem an exceptionally urgent one, actually one almost of survival.

Historically, the first and most dramatic result of the mass influx of non-western children into a western-type educational system was extremely widespread school failure. One became accustomed to the fact that while non-western children comprised 60 percent of school entrants, only 25 percent of those who were graduated from primary school at the end of the eighth grade were

non-western. Moreover, during these early years only 12 percent of high
school students were of non-western parentage.

As in other countries, the initial teaching of reading proved to be the major
stumbling block; and for a few years it was quite usual to find that by the end
of their first year in school, nearly half the pupils of a class had failed to learn
to read (2). A very dramatic change in attitude on the part of the educational authorities occurred in the wake of a small number of action studies
which demonstrated that once teaching methods are adapted to the special
characteristics of the non-western child, educational achievements are drastical-
ly improved (1). While at first efforts at developing new teaching strategies
were sporadic and not coordinated, a central agency for the planning and implementation of all such efforts was set up by 1963.

A Framework for Compensatory Education

In 1963 the Ministry of Education and Culture established the Center for
Schools in Need of Nurture* with the defined aim of " ... planning and implementing compensatory programs in order to help pupils of non-western
parents to cope successfully with the demands of the Israeli school system".

Underlying this definition was the firm conviction, based on experience,
that efficient compensatory action could indeed bring about drastic improvements. As in its definition, so in its work, the Center for Schools in Need of
Nurture (or in short is based on an interaction between theory and practice.
The N. N.) basic administrative policy is that the more needs a specific school
has, the more services or nurture it should have. According to this policy,
points are alloted to primary schools in accordance with three criteria:

1. *Performance of the pupils on national examinations which are administered on the fourth- and eigth-grade level.* The poorer the pupils of a
   given school perform on these examinations, the more points the school
   will get.
2. *Teacher qualifications.* Inexperienced teachers, poorly qualified teachers,
   and teachers who commute to the schools in which they teach, all add
   points to their school.
3. *Home background of the pupils.* Parents who immigrated from Middle
   Eastern countries, little formal education on the parts of the parents, a
   foreign language spoken in the home, and the unavailability of help for
   school assignments are all factors which are translatable into points allotted to a given school.

Schools which receive a certain number of points or more are officially designated as N. N. schools and entitled to the full range of benefits worked out

---

* The author is grateful to Sylvia Krown of the Ministry of Health for suggesting
this term as an appropriate translation of the Hebrew name.

for these schools. The following abridged list will give an idea of the type and range of benefits available:

1. Smaller classes.
2. An eleven-month school year and a prolonged school day.
3. Intensive group coaching in basic subjects in the sixth, seventh, and eighth grades.
4. Special educational consultants who meet regularly with teachers of the first four grades as well as special teaching manuals and training sessions for these teachers.
5. Remedial teachers or reading specialists attached to the schools.
6. After-school-hours enrichment centers for promising pupils to prepare them for high school.
7. Special teaching strategies and experimentation, developmentation, and implementation of textbooks and instructional materials.

At present a third of all primary schools have been officially designated as N. N. schools and consequently entitled to the compensatory programs described as well as additional programs in some instances.

A further 10 percent of all primary schools get some of the described benefits despite the fact that they were not recognized officially as N. N. schools.

Inservice Training for Compensatory Education

As stated, an intensive inservice training program for the teachers in the lower grades of N. N. schools is one of the benefits accruing to these schools. On the other hand, it must be remembered that the poor training of these teachers and/or their degree of inexperience were contributing factors in establishing the school as an N. N. school. While it is true that the teachers of the lower grades in these schools get intensive inservice training, these teachers are also the ones who need it most. The inservice training can take three forms and most usually combines them all:

1. Special educational consultants are assigned to small groups of teachers. This consultant, usually an experienced and successful teacher, meets her teachers individually once every fortnight and helps them plan their work in detail. She also frequently visits their classrooms.

Groups of two or three consultants are also active in devising new teaching approaches and materials and guiding the teachers in experimenting with them.

2. Special manuals are issued several times each school year. New teaching approaches and devices are described in these manuals in great detail. Furthermore, many practical hints about planning and carrying out successful projects are offered.

3. Intensive inservice training sessions are arranged during school holidays. In these sessions the newly developed materials are introduced to larger audiences, including also teachers in non N. N. schools.

While during school sessions the link of an individual teacher to the many-faceted work of the Center for N. N. Schools is mainly through her consultant and through the manuals, school holidays are utilized for broader contacts and concentrated training. This link also allows for the opportunity of teachers to hear about work beyond their immediate concern.

Preservice Training for Compensatory Education

While inservice training programs are well developed and extensive, and there is good reason to believe that the new educational practices which are developed experimentally for the N. N. schools will eventually come to the attention of the practicing teacher, the area of preservice training has so far remained largely untouched. Two sets of factors are mainly responsible for this situation:

First, there is the normal time lag between educational innovation and its introduction into the curricula of teacher-traning institutions. It seems reasonable to assume that the teachers in teacher-training institutions usually received their own training and, furthermore, have taught in the school system before the creation of the Center for N. N. Schools — sometimes even before mass immigration ever began.

Second, there is the often-voiced assumption that training teachers for compensatory educational work cannot be successfully achieved in the initial stages of teacher training. The proponents of this view would hold that a person must first receive his basic training which "makes him a teacher" and that the additional knowledge and skills needed for compensatory work can be successfully assimilated only if they are superimposed on this already existing "teacher".

Much further study in this controversial area is clearly needed, and the position which will be presented in this paper is at present no more than a personal statement unsubstantiated by methodical research.

It hardly seems logical that once new teaching methods have been developed and widely accepted, they should not be part of the initial training of new teachers, especially since in this area, as so often happened in other areas, these new methods are already exerting considerable influence on teaching practices in all schools.

The writer feels that a further substantiation of her stand can be drawn from the Proceedings of the New York State Education Department Conference on College and University Programs for Teachers of the Disadvantaged, which was held in 1967 (4). A large number of the participants at this conference stressed the importance of adequate preservice training as an essential step in the preparation of future teachers of the disadvantaged for the special conditions they will have to face.

But it would be a mistake to think of training teachers for work in N. N. schools only in terms of a training in the use of additional teaching strategies and devices. This paper opened with a discussion of cultural diversity. The basic fact of the problem under consideration is surely that of pupils whose cultural background is different from that of their teachers.

Several American educators referred to this problem in writing about the preparation of teachers for work with the disadvantaged, concluding that teachers in training should learn about the anthropological and sociological background of their future charges in order to prevent the "culture shock" in store for the teacher upon being first exposed to this reality (4).

Yet it seems that theoretical "knowledge about the child in his environment", as prescribed for instance by Miriam Goldberg for the "Successful Teacher of Disadvantaged Pupils" (3), is too superficial an approach. An understanding of an alien culture cannot be acquired by book learning alone. In 1964 Riessman and Hannah wrote:

> The beginning solution, it seems to us, must stem from our teacher traning institutions. We must work out a whole new system of pedagogy geared to the teaching of children from low-income families. Larger doses of sociological and anthropological material must be dispensed to teacher trainees in order to develop an appreciation of other ways of living, other realities.
>
> Concurrently, there should be community field trips, home visits and student teaching in a variety of situations. Teachers should find out what it is like to eat rice and beans every day on a welfare budget, how it feels to wait five hours in a city clinic before being seen, why a family would choose to have a television set before a second pair of shoes all around (9).

In order to be able to react effectively within a framework of basic differences in cultural background and outlook, the teacher must have experienced these differences firsthand.

At Hebrew University the writer and others have been experimenting with applying to the exigencies of cultural diversity some aspects of the child-study program developed by Prescott and his coworkers at the University of Maryland (8). Every year, so far, we have learned again that only at the stage when students have experienced the everyday conditions and problems of the children's homes, does the desired understanding and change in attitude occur. These results were, in many cases, encouraging beyond fondest hopes. Still it has to be remembered that these field experiences followed a period of theoretical preparation.

Conclusion

In the forties, Allison David in his classic works described the problems arising out of the discrepancy between the home background of large segments of pupils and the school. Unless teachers-in-training are introduced to these differences via a well-planned program including firsthand field experience, there is little hope that the necessary changes will be achieved in the near future. It should be remembered that present teacher training is still often based on the assumption of a uniform society in which the home background of future pupils is known to the teacher-in-training because it essentially resembles his own. Only when the vast change in this respect has been fully taken into account and teachers have a firsthand knowledge of the details of their charges' home environment, is there hope that teachers will be able to react naturally and competently to the special demands evolving from these basic differences in the everyday teaching situation. A well-planned preservice training based on anthropological theory combined with intensive field experience in families and community institutions seems the most hopeful approach for breaching the cultural gap between teacher and pupil.

REFERENCES

1. Dror, R. "Educational Research in Israel", in *Scripta Hierosolymitana* 13, Jerusalem, Magnes Press, 1963.
2. Feitelson, D. *The Causes of School Failure Among First Graders,* Jerusalem, The Henrietta Szold Foundation, 1953 (in Hebrew).
3. Goldberg, M. L. "Adapting Teacher Style to Pupil Differences: Teachers for Disadvantaged Children", *Merrill—Palmer Quarterly* (April 1964), 161—178.
4. Jablonsky, A. (Ed.). *Imperatives for Change,* Proceedings of the New York State Education Department Conference on College and University Programs for Teachers of the Disadvantaged, April 10—11, 1967. New York, Yeshiva University, 1967.
5. Kaplan, B. A. "Issues in Educating the Culturally Disadvantaged", *Phi Delta Kappan* (November 1963), 70—76.
6. Klopf, G. J., and G. W. Bowman. *Teacher Education in a Social Context.* New York: Bank Street College of Education, 1966.
7. Mackler, B. "The Civil Rights Movement: From Reflection to Heartbreak", *Teachers College Record* 68 (1966), 42—48.
8. Prescott, D. A. *The Child in the Educative Process.* New York: McGraw—Hill, 1957.
9. Riessman, F., and A. Hannah. "Teachers of the Poor", *The PTA Magazine* (November 1964), 12—14.

RONALD W. MITCHELL

INTERNATIONAL READING ASSOCIATION
NEWARK, DELAWARE
UNITED STATES OF AMERICA

The ERIC/CRIER Research Retrieval and Dissemination Center

FOR THE PAST SEVERAL YEARS the educational community has been experiencing an ever-increasing flow of research literature. Researchers, stimulated by government and private foundation funds, using the latest, most sophisticated techniques have been attacking problems at an accelerating pace. In order for the knowledge and insights gained from these studies to be useful, however, the information must reach the teachers, administrators, directors, and other researchers concerned with education.

Confronted with this tremendous influx of information, even the most accomplished researcher faces an almost insurmountable task. He must not only survey the literature published in educational journals but must seek out the fugitive material — the unpublished colloquium papers and doctorial dissertations, the papers presented at conventions, and the ever-increasing work being done by independent school systems.

ERIC

In an attempt to bring some organization to the research field, the United States Office of Education (USOE) in 1966 established the Educational Resources Information Center commonly referred to by the acronym ERIC. The basic functions of this information system are the retrieval, collection, storage, reduction, analysis, and dissemination of educational information.

ERIC is a rather unique system in that it combines a centralized and decentralized organizational format. Central ERIC, located in Washington, D. C., governs and coordinates the work of eighteen special clearinghouses, each representing different disciplines within the area of education. These clearinghouses are located at universities and other educational institutions across the United States.

Each clearinghouse is staffed by specialists in a respective area of education.

These experts collect, select, abstract, and index materials for inclusion in the ERIC system. Each clearinghouse also acts as a fairly independent retrieval, analysis, and dissemination center within its particular discipline. Its sources of material are the published and unpublished literature plus reports on government-sponsored projects filtered to the respective clearinghouses by ERIC Central.

When a clearinghouse receives a document, the material is first evaluated to determine its significance. If the document is selected for inclusion in the ERIC system, the clearinghouse indexes the material by use of established descriptors, such as Phonics, Inservice Teacher Education, Educable Mentally Handicapped, and so forth. Each document may be described by several such descriptors. An abstract is then prepared and is forwarded to ERIC Central along with the descriptors and, in most cases, the full document.

Research in Education

At ERIC Central the document is assigned an Ed number and announced in the USOE publication, *Research in Education* (RIE). This publication is available in many libraries or may be ordered by individuals for $11 per year for subscribers in the United States and $13 for those in other countries. The second price listed implies, of course, that ERIC resources are available to educators throughout the world. A yearly subscription including twelve issues may be ordered from

> Superintendent of Documents
> United States Government Printing Office
> Washington, D.C. 20402
> U.S.A.

The listing of a document in RIE includes the Ed number, the descriptors, and the abstract. By consulting the descriptors, the user can isolate the reports of studies of interest. Then, by reading the selected abstracts, the user can decide whether he wishes to order the complete document. The cost of the complete document, both in microfiche (MF) and hard copy (HC), is indicated in the listing.

To order the document, the user must contact

> ERIC Document Reproduction Service
> National Cash Register, Inc.
> 4936 Fairmont Avenue
> Bethesda, Maryland 20014
> U.S.A.

Documents should be ordered by Ed number.

Microfiche versus Hard Copy

It might be wise at this point to discuss briefly microfiche and hard copy, the two forms in which materials may be ordered from EDRS. Microfiche, a 4 × 6-inch sheet of microfilm, may contain up to seventy pages of printed material. The cost of each 4 × 6 sheet is currently about twenty-five cents.

Hard copy refers to Xerox copies produced in 6 × 8-inch sheets. The cost is four cents per page or $2.80 for a seventy-page document. The cost of microfiche is, therefore, substantially below that of hard copy; however, to read the microfiche one must have special equipment called a microfiche reader. These readers range in price from $75 to $1400. The hard copy, of course, may be read without the aid of special equipment.

Levels of Input

Actually it is not always possible to retrieve microfiche or hard copies from ERIC for every document listed in RIE. If printed copies of the material are readily available to the user from some other source. ERIC may offer the original document only in microfiche. If the material is covered by a copyright, the original document will not be available in either MF or HC. In both cases the materials are listed in RIE because ERIC feels that the educational community should be alerted to the document's existence and be directed to the source from which the material may be ordered.

ERIC/CRIER

Each month, Indiana University receives letters addressed to Mr. ERIC CRIER or Dr. CRIER. There is, of course, no such person on the staff. ERIC/CRIER is the acronym for the ERIC Clearinghouse on Retrieval of Information and Evaluation on Reading. This clearinghouse is guided by Leo Fay and Edward Summers, the project directors, with the help of an advisory board made up of some of the leading experts in the field of reading. The clearinghouse, supported by the U. S. Office of Education, is cosponsored by Indiana University and the International Reading Association (IRA).

ERIC/CRIER has the primary responsibility of inputting material from the field of reading into the ERIC system. Each month ERIC/CRIER receives many manuscripts dealing with some aspect of reading from individual researchers or teachers. The material is carefully screened, and descriptors and an abstract are prepared for those documents selected for input. The information on the selected documents is then forwarded to ERIC Central and usually appears in RIE within three months.

In addition to announcing these original materials through the ERIC system, ERIC/CRIER also creates new documents, such as bibliographies, reviews of the research, and state-of-the-art papers.

ERIC/CRIER receives several requests from individuals for information on certain topics, such as phonics or reading readiness. It would, of course, be impossible to run an extensive search of all of the materials filed at ERIC/CRIER everytime an individual request is received. In an attempt to handle such requests, however, ERIC/CRIER is developing bibliographies and reviews of the literature in several areas. As a bibliography or review becomes available, it is announced through a continuing ERIC/CRIER column in the three journals of the International Reading Association. Its availability is also announced in RIE.

In addition to these smaller bibliographies limited to specific areas within the field of reading, ERIC/CRIER has prepared a general annotated bibliography of the published research in reading from 1900—1966. This bibliography, developed from the famous Gray collection of published research housed at the University of Chicago, is published in three volumes:

Published Research Literature in Reading, 1900—1949
Published Research Literature in Reading, 1950—1963
Published Research Literature in Reading, 1964—1966

The total cost of all three volumes would be $4.25 in microfiche and about $43 in hard copy.

Reading Review Series

One of the most recent developments at ERIC/CRIER is the establishment of the Reading Review Series. Here, an expert in a particular area of reading, such as reading at the high school level, is asked not only to review the literature in this area but also to summarize and interpret it — What do we know? Where do we stand? Where are we going? The author is provided with all materials available in the ERIC/CRIER files to facilitate his work and insure complete coverage of his topic.

The first two manuscripts are being published through the International Reading Association Research Fund. They will also be available in microfiche from the ERIC system. One of these papers covers the area of high school reading. It was prepared by A. Sterl Artley of the University of Missouri. The other, on the diagnosis and treatment of reading disabilities, was written by Ruth Strang of the University of Arizona. Everyone who has reviewed the manuscripts thus far has suggested that they are outstanding contributions to the field of reading.

Access to the ERIC System

The easiest way to gain access to the ERIC and the ERIC/CRIER facilities is to write directly to

> ERIC/CRIER
> 200 Pine Hall
> Indiana University
> Bloomington, Indiana 47401
> U.S.A.

One may obtain from that office a pamphlet titled "Portfolio of ERIC and ERIC/CRIER Products and Services". This portfolio describes in detail all materials mentioned plus several other products and services. It also contains information on microfiche readers.

In addition to the portfolio, one may request information on specific topics. If bibliographies or reviews are available, ERIC/CRIER will send the information necessary for ordering the documents.

Be sure to consult the three IRA journals also. The ERIC/CRIER column will contain announcements of new developments and materials.

Finally, as the user becomes familiar with the system, he may wish to subscribe to *Research in Education*. The portfolio from ERIC/CRIER contains directions for securing RIE from ERIC Central.

Conclusion

The ERIC system is very new. It has not yet reached its maximum efficiency, for its potentials are tremendous. The staff at ERIC/CRIER hopes that all educators will make use of the present system and, by making suggestions, contribute to the development of an even more sophisticated informational retrieval and dissemination network.

READING PROBLEMS

Andrée Piacere

REEDUCATOR PSYCHO-PEDAGOGICAL
and

Jean Piacere

SCHOOL PSYCHOLOGIST
PARIS

Integration Speed-Accuracy to a test of crossing signs by children poor in reading.

The study of the integration speed-accuracy and the modalities of the visual exploration of a group of children poor in reading, to a test of crossing signs, allows, on non-linguistic material, to cast some light on the special difficulties shown by the subjects to grasp and to recognize a series of meaningless graphical structures, presented to them on a continuous and systematized speed.

The poor readers are found inferior to the general population mainly in accuracy. A later distinction between "common poor readers" and "pathological readers", on the basis of their scholastic behavior, allows moreover, to draw on these two subgroups behaviors differentiated in speed and efficiency accompanying ways of diversely disorganized visual exploration.

The clinical study of some cases of poor readers belonging to the same or to different families, confirms the parallelism which exists between behaviors during the test of crossing signs on individuals having the same lexical comportment.

On the other hand the behavior of the poor reader does not seem to be assimilable neither to the mentally retarded, nor to the youngest children participating in the same tests.

This study allows us to verify the role of the energizing factors of mobilization, of focalization and control of attention as well as possibilities of integration of speed-accuracy, all involved in the reading concurrently with the symbolic function.

ANDRÉE PIACERE

RÉEDUCATRICE PSYCHO-PÉDAGOGIQUE
et

JEAN PIACERE

PSYCHOLOGUE SCOLAIRE
PARIS

Integration vitesse-precision a une epreuve de barrage de signes chez les enfants mauvais lecteurs

I Position du probleme et buts de la recherche

L'acte de lecture peut être considéré comme un processus complexe de transformations et d'intégrations successives qui, portant sur un message écrit, permettent d'accéder à la signification dont il est porteur. D'une manière plus spécifique c'est une activité de décodage appliquée au domaine linguistique. De ce fait la lecture fait appel à des activités mentales et à des comportements plus ou moins élaborés, tels l'intelligence assurant la compréhension, la fonction symbolique permettant l'utilisation des codes linguistiques (code phonétique et code graphique), la perception des unités du message constitué ici par une suite ordonnée de signes graphiques. Tous ces processus étant liés par un jeu d'intégrations mutuelles assurées par le système nerveux central, selon des modalités d'ailleurs variables en fonction des situations de lecture, des niveaux d'apprentissage et de personnalité du sujet lisant.

Il est maintenant bien connu que l'acte de lire engage, à des titres diverse, des aspects variés de la personnalité, depuis l'équipement sensoriel et cognitif du sujet jusqu'à son affectivité et sa motivation.

Notre recherche, qui s'inscrit dans l'étude de la personnalité des mauvais lecteurs, s'attache à deux aspects du comportement lexique encore insuffisamment explorés: l'autorégulation des variables vitesse et précision qui se situe principalement au niveau de l'exploration perceptive du message, et, secondairement, l'attitude énergétique du sujet durant l'activité exploratoire du texte qui constitue beaucoup plus un trait de personnalité globale.

a/ *L'intégration vitesse-précision.*

Si la faute de lecture (ou mieux l'erreur de décodage) est, à des degrés divers, le lot de tous les lecteurs pourvu qu'ils lisent assez longtemps un texte difficile et qu'il faille renoncer à découvrir des types de "fautes" véritablement spécifiques de la dyslexie (P. LEFAVRAIS. M. LOBROT) il n'en reste pas moins que l'on s'accorde généralement pour reconnaître, dans le cas de la lecture orale, le mauvais lecteur du bon lecteur par le style de leur lecture. L'impression de mauvaise lecture est donnée par la lenteur, l'irrégularité du débit et la densité des erreurs, le tout compromettant plus ou moins la communication du message du lecteur à l'auditeur. Vitesse, nombre d'erreurs et qualité du débit étant les 3 variables classiquement utilisées, isolément ou conjointement, dans les tests de lecture orale. Chez la majorité des sujets il s'établit, dans la lecture courante d'un texte de lisibilité moyenne, une auto-régulation entre la vitesse et la précision de telle manière que le nombre d'erreurs de lecture, reste compatible avec une compréhnsion suffisante du message par le lecteur lui-même. (P. LEFAVRAIS). C'est pourquoi la seule mesure de la vitesse est généralement une bonne appréciation de l'efficience en lecture, passé le stade des premiers apprentissages, indice utilisé dans de nombreux test. Par contre il est des cas où cet auto-ajustement automatique ne s'établit pas et où les rapports vitesse-exactitude et vitesse-compréhension deviennent inconstants. Cela se produit chez le débutant qui n'est pas encore arrivé à la lecture courante, occasionnellement chez tout lecteur même bon, aux prises avec un texte mal adapté à ses possibilités (trop facile la vitesse est en quelque sorte libérée du souci de précision, trop difficile le nombre de fautes tend à croître alors même que la vitesse diminue), et d'une manière constante chez le mauvais lecteur qui nous intéresse ici, parce que, pratiquement, tout texte écrit lui est inadapté.

b/ *Le potentiel énergétique.*

La nature même du message écrit exige que soient respectées certaines règles dans son exploration pour en permettre un décodage efficace : exploration visuelle sans omission dans un sens donné : gauche-droite et ligne par ligne dans notre système usuel d'écriture. Cette exploration exige une stabilité visuelle, une aisance de repérage, une focalisation de l'attention suffisantes, dont tous les lecteurs ne sont pas également capables avec constance et régularité : il n'est que de voir combien de jeunes enfants ont de mal à ne pas sauter de ligne, la tendance de certains débutants à inverser le sens de la lecture et à s'aider du doigt pour soutenir leur contrôle visuel. Dissociée de l'aspect précision, la vitesse de lecture, bien que variable génétique, devient, en quelque manière, tout comme le débit du discours, un trait individuel de personnalité.

c/ *Lecture et barrage de signes.*

Dans l'hypothèse donc où la mauvaise lecture se caractérise entre autres, par une perturbation de l'équilibre vitesse/précision compromettant chez le lecteur lui-même, et en tout cas chez l'auditeur, l'accès à la signification du message, et où cette perturbation peut s'accompagner d'une désorganisation de l'exploration visuelle du texte écrit, il devenait tentant d'étudier sur un matériel non linguistique, tel l'épreuve du barrage de signes, le comportement exploratoire et l'efficience des mauvais lecteurs.

Nous ne considèrerons évidemment pas que lecture et barrage de signes soient deux tâches équivalentes. La lecture beaucoup plus complexe, fait intervenir des fonctions qu'ignore le barrage: fonction symbolique, linguistique, fonction de communication elle exige un apprentissage long, la connaissance d'un code de 26 signes ainsi que la maîtrise de leurs multiples combinaisons, alors qu'il suffit de quelques secondes pour assimiler les consignes du barrage.

Toutefois la comparaison de ces deux tâches se justifie en ce sens qu'elles mettent en jeu un comportement d'exploration visuelle systématisé servant de support à une activité mentale de reconnaissance de signes graphiques linéairement disposés, et dont la vitesse, la précision et le rendement sont mesurables.

Il est donc possible pour des groupes de sujets, voire pour un même sujet, d'établir une comparaison entre les performances analogues réalisées aux deux tâches, de façon à vérifier l'existence de comportements spécifiques dans le domaine de l'efficience énergétique et du pouvoir de contrôle à des niveaux divers.

II La population d'experience

Il s'agit uniquement de sujets d'âge scolaire reconnus *mauvais lecteurs* à la fois d'après le jugement des maîtres et d'après leurs résultats aux tests de lecture, se répartissant ainsi:

30 garçons et 30 filles âgés de 6;10 à 13;4 dont le QI moyen est de 93,7 (60 à 120) avec un retard de lecture 1 à 6 ans.

● Ces élèves ont été recrutés:

1963 — II dans un centre médico-psycho-pédagogique (9 G—2 F) QI moyen 100

1964 à 67—34 dans les classes normales d'un groupe scolaire de la banlieue de PARIS (22 F. 12 G. QI moyen 90,7)

1967 — 15 élèves d'une classe spéciale de Réadaptation (6 F 9 g. QI moyen 90,5)

Il s'agit donc d'enfants ayant tous reçu, sinon assimilé, les apprentissages de base qui auraient dû, normalement, leur permettre de dépasser le seuil de la lecture courante. Cet échantillon assez hétérogène en ce qui concerne l'âge, le niveau mental, l'origine socio-économique, rassemble toutefois bien que dans des proportions non contrôlées, les principaux types de mauvais lecteurs qu'on-peut rencontrer à ce niveau de population scolaire.

III Les épreuves utilisées

Chacun des 60 sujets a subi successivement un test de lecture et une épreuve de barrage de signes.

a/ *Les épreuves de lecture:*

Deux tests de lecture ont été utilisés selon les enfants:

"René" test de lecture orale de *J.* BURION (Institut supérieur de Pédagogie du Hainaut. MORLANWELZ (BELGIQUE)

Épreuve de lecture suivie, de difficulté progressive qui, utilisée avec l'étalonnage parisien réalisé par *M.* GILLY permet l'établissement d'un niveau de lecture de la IIéme (cours préparatoire) à la 9éme (cours élémentaire 2éme année). Ce test est étalonné en fonction d'un indice de rendement intégrant à la fois la vitesse et la précision.

"L'Alouette" test d'analyse de la lecture et de la dyslexie de *P. LEFAVRAIS* C. P. A. PARIS, conçu pour pouvoir être utilisé à tous les niveaux de lecture de la IIème classe à l'âge adulte. Il permet, outre la possibilité d'une analyse qualitative et étiologique des fautes, l'établissement d'un niveau apparent de lecture qui ne tient compte que de la vitesse et d'un niveau de lecture réel qui, tenant de l'exatitude constitue un indice de rendement.

Dans la mesure où il ne s'agissait pas d'établir des catégorisations fines mais essentiellement de discriminer des mauvais lecteurs, l'utilisation conjointe de ces deux épreuves ne présentait pas d'inconvénient majeur.

b/ *L'épreuve de barrage de signes*

Nous avons utilisé le *double barrage* T2 B, mis au point par René ZAZZO (1) qui se déroule à deux niveaux de complexité:

— Au 1er barrage, le sujet doit barrer en temps libre sur une feuille de 1 000 signes carrés tous ceux d'un modèle donné.

• — Au second barrage, sur une feuille similaire, il lui faut barrer simultanément deux types de carrés, épreuve d'attention distribuée à poursuivre durant 10 minutes d'affilée.

Dans les deux cas la même consigne est donnée au sujet de travailler ''vite et bien'', mettant l'accent à la fois et également sur l'exigence de vitesse et de précision.

L'enregistrement des données en cours d'épreuve porte à la fois sur les aspects quantitatifs et qualitatifs du comportement. Leur dépouillement permet le calcul d'un certain nombre d'indices concernant la vitesse, la précision et le rendement et, par référence à des valeurs expérimentales, l'établissement d'une formule résumant l'essentiel du comportement du sujet.

Il est donc possible, sur la base du T2B d'étudier, statistiquement au niveau du groupe et cliniquement au niveau de l'individu, l'intégration vitesse précision à deux niveaux d'activité exploratoire visuelle, et d'analyser plus finement les variations d'efficience aux divers moments de l'épreuve.

IV Methodologie

N'ayant pu, faute de temps, examiner que des enfants mauvais lecteurs, nous avons pris comme normes de référence les performances de l'échantillon de 350 écoliers parisiens de 8 à 14 ans, utilisé par R. ZAZZO pour étalonner le T2B. Nous avons estimé légitime d'admettre qu'en tant qu'échantillon au hazard il était également représentatif en ce qui concerne la lecture, et pouvait nous servir valablement de groupe témoin.

Du fait de cette limitation, et de l'étendue restreinte de nos effectifs, la présente études ne constitue, selon nous, qu'une première approche des problèmes.

Par ailleurs, nos effectifs par sexe et âge étant trop réduits pour autoriser des comparaisons de moyennes, nous avons choisi, pour chacune des 3 variables étudiées, de classer nos sujets selon une trichotomie du type lents, moyens, rapides, définie en fonction de l'écart semi inter quartile de chaque âge, selon le modèle utilisé par R. ZAZZO. Ce procédé, qui neutralise la variable âge permet la construction de tables de contingence auxquelles peuvent être appliqués la statistique du χ^2 et ses dérivés.

Resultats

Iere partie: Comparaison globale des performances des mauvais lecteurs à celles de la population générale.

Nous avons analysé successivement le rendement global et ses deux composantes, la vitesse et la précision, à chacun des deux barrages isolément puis conjointement.

a) *étude du rendement:* à aucun des 2 barrages il n'existe de différence significative entre mauvais lecteurs, filles ou garçons et les enfants du groupe témoin.

b) *étude de la vitesse:* même conclusion que pour le rendement. Si l'on compare pour chacune des zones de vitesse (L—M—R·) la proportion de sujets constants ou inconstants, on constate chez les mauvais lecteurs une tendance très significative (S à .01) à garder le même style de vitesse aux 2

(1) Manuel pour l'examen psychologique de l'enfant. — fasc. 7 — Delachaux Niestlé.

barrages, ce qui rejoint la corrélation positive de .57 trouvée par Roger
PERRON (Manuel p. 253).

c) *étude de la précision,* seule variable pour laquelle R. ZAZZO a constaté
quelque différence entre garçons et filles, bien que nonsignificative au
niveau de l'étalonnage.

Au barrage d'un signe les garçons mauvais lecteurs comme ceux du groupe
témoin, sont plus souvent exacts qu'inexacts (S à .025). Inversement les
mauvaises lectrices, ayant une faible tendance à être plutôt inexactes (S
à .10), se distinguent des filles du groupe témoin (S à .01) qui sont le
plus souvent exactes.

Au barrage de deux signes, alors que G. et F (du groupe témoin sont plus
souvent exacts qu'inexacts (S très sup. à .0005), les G. d'ailleurs bien
plus que les filles (S à .025), chez les mauvais lecteurs G. et F. sont aussi
souvent inexacts qu'exacts. De ce fait, si les mauvaises lectrices se différencient peu des filles du groupe témoin, les garçons mauvais lecteurs sont
beaucoup moins précis que les garçons tout venant (S à .01).

Chez les mauvais lecteurs, garçons et filles se comportent différemment
du groupe témoin, et différemment aussi les uns des autres selon le niveau
de complexité de la tâche. *Les garçons,* le plus souvent exacts à BI,
comme les normaux, enregistrent à B2 une chute de la précision, contrairement à ceux du groupe témoin (S à .01). Inversement, *les filles mauvaises
lectrices,* moins exactes à B1 que celles du groupe témoin (S à .01), ob-
tiennent une amélioration relative à B2 qui les rapproche de ces dernières
(NS à .05).

Si nous considérons *l'évolution de la précision aux deux barrages à la
fois,* il existe chez les mauvais lecteurs, et surtout chez les filles, une tendance significative à être inexact à B1 et à B2 (S à .01).

Ceux des mauvais lecteurs dont la précision est inconstante se comportent différemment selon le sexe: chez les garçons la précision tend à se
détériorer à B2 (contrairement au gr. témoin) alors que chez les filles elle
tend à s'améliorer.

d) *relation vitesse: précision*

Par ailleurs, comme dans la population témoin, chez les mauvais lecteurs, G ou F, les sujets imprécis ont tendance à se trouver plus nombreux
chez les lents et les rapides:

63 % des lents, 43 % des moyens, 60 % des rapides sont imprecis.

e) *Un mode atypique d'exploration visuelle: le boustrophédon.*

Il s'agit du recours systématique ou occasionnel à l'exploration des lignes
alternativement selon le sens G/D—D/G, qui facilite considérablement
le répérage, du début de ligne.

Ce comportement exploratoire, très minoritaire dans le groupe témoin, est adopté par près du tiers des mauvais lecteurs :

		B1	B2	B1/B2	Total
groupe témoin	350 sujets	3,7 %	2,3 %	6 %	12 %
mauvais lect.	60 sujets	3,3 %	3,3 %	20 %	27 %

(S à .01)

Les M. L. recourant au boustrophédon se trouvent plus souvent que les autres en survitesse à B2 (V>V1 et In2 éléve) On trouve parmi eux 44 % de formules en U (11,75 % dans le gr. témoin) Ils sont aussi plus inexacts que les M. L. à l'exploration G. D (S à .01).

f) *Formules de travail anormales.* —

Il s'agit des formules qui, dans la population générale, traduisent l'inhibition (formules en LE) ou au contraire l'impulsivité, le manque de contrôle (formules en RU, excepté RU. I obtenu par les sujets très doués capables à la fois d'une vitesse élevée et d'une bonne précision aux deux barrages).

Si les formules caractéristiques de l'inhibition ne sont guère plus nombreuses chez les mauvais lecteurs que dans le groupe témoin, celles traduisant impulsivité et manque de contrôle y sont plus fréquentes (6 % contre 3 %) et s'y trouvent toujours associées à un mauvais indice d'exactitude. (6 % de RU4, RU5, RU6 contre 2 % dans le groupe témoin).

Conclusion

C'est donc surtout en ce qui concerne la précision que les mauvais lecteurs se trouvent être inférioris és par rapport aux autres élèves. Les garçons mauvais lecteurs s'adaptent moins bien que les filles mauvaises lectrices quand la tâche devient plus complexe, alors que pour ces dernières c'est le Ier barrage, pourtant le plus facile, qui provoque le plus d'erreurs. Ceci peut s'expliquer aussi bien par une réaction émotive initiale à la situation de testing que par une plus grande lenteur de mobilisation chez les mauvaises lectrices.

En outre, les difficultés d'adaptation à une activité d'exploration visuelle systématisée particulières aux mauvais lecteurs sont confirmées par leurs recours plus fréquents que les autres enfants à des comportements atypiques (boustrophédon).

2ème partie: Comparaison de deux groupes de mauvais lecteurs.

Nous avons distingué, dans notre échantillon de mauvais lecteurs, deux catégories de sujets selon leurs performances au test de lecture et leur comportement scolaire général : les "simples mauvais lecteurs" dont l'échec en lecture est limité et ne retentit pas notablement sur les autres apprentissages, et les lecteurs dits "pathologiques", dont la lecture reste en deçà du seuil d'utilisation pratique, avec un rendement scolaire global sévèrement perturbé (15 élèves, dont II G. et 4 F.).

Du point de vue de la précision "simples mauvais lecteurs" et "lecteurs pathologiques" ne se différencient pas significativement. Pour la vitesse il n'en est pas de même, car les "lecteurs pathologiques" sont le plus souvent très lents :

simples M.L.	24,4 %	lents	46,6	moyens	29	% rapides
lect. pathol.	53,3 %		33	%	13,7 %	

Sign à .05 à B1 et à .01 à B2

Si l'ensemble des mauvais lecteurs se différencie du groupe témoin par son inexactitude, le sous-groupe des "lecteurs pathologiques" s'en distingue en outre par sa lenteur. Il s'ensuit donc que leur rendement est doublement inférioirisé.

3ème partie : monographies cliniques parallèles de mauvais lecteurs.
A-Etude longitudinale comparée de deux fratries de mauvaislecteurs.

+*fratrie LAL*   famille normale de 10 enfants. de niveau socio-culturel médiocre, pathogène et formant des personnalités schizoïdes, car très refermés sur elle-même.
4 sujets suivis (2 F. et 2 G.) retard de développement mental (fausse débilité) et staturo-pondéral, puis tendance à obésité; bonne santé et bonne fréquentation scolaire. Placés en classe spéciale car rendement scolaire très faible dans le domaine du langage écrit: pour trois d'entre eux, lecture et orthographe pathologiques confinant à l'alexie.

+*fratrie MARG.*   famille de 6 enfants, fruste mais bien adaptée socialement présentant tous un retard scolaire. QI entre 85 et 100.
3 sujets suivis (2 F et 1 G.), enfants sains, solides, sans absentéisme. Difficultés de lecture dues à un mauvais contrôle vitesse/précision et à un retard linguistique socio-culturel ("simples mauvais lect.").

Ne pouvant ici présenter le détail de l'anamnèse et du comportement aux tests de chacun des sujets, nous ne ferons que dégager les grands traits qui les caractérisent ou les opposent de fratrie à fratrie au barrage.

— Chaque fratrie a son *style de vitesse* qui se maintient d'ailleurs d'âge en âge: lent chez les LAL (lect. pathologiques), rapide chez les MARG. (simples M. L.). Il semble s'agir là d'une caractéristique familiale constitutionnelle.

— *La précision* semble davantage être une caractéristique individuelle, bien que la majorité des sujets soient imprécis dans les deux fratries.

— *L'intégration vitesse/précision* est assez satisfaisante, bien qu'effectuée à bas régime, chez les 3 lecteurs pathologiques de la famille LAL, chez qui le rendement moyen est très faible pour leur âge réel et la courbe de travail reste infantile. Chez les "simples M. L." que sont les MARG., au contraire, le style de travail est beaucoup plus mûr le rendement moyen satisfaisant, mais l'adaptation vitesse/précision plus variable, l'accent étant mis sur la vitesse.

B1Etude de deux enfants de classe de réadaptation

+ S.M. — fillette de 7;5, Q.I. 93; fatigable, instabile et dispersée avec problèmes névrotiques. Lecture rapide au rendement de 6;6 à 6;9 — exploration anarchique du texte, mots et lignes sautées, erreur nombreuses.

+ D.C. — garçon de 8;8 Q.I. 78; fatigable, instable, signes d'ambryopathie discrets, trouble du langage parlé rééduqué, relation enfant-parents médiocre. Lecture lente, assez peu précise de niveau 7 ans.

Le barrage présente chez ces deux sujets des indices d'un déficit considérable du contrôle de l'attention et qui confirment leur instabilité: désorganisation du mode d'exploration (lignes sautées, boustrophédon), survitesse et forte imprécision au 2ème barrage (71 % d'erreurs chez la fille, 51 % chez le garçon), similitude des formules, à la vitesse près (RU5 chez la fille, LU5 chez le G.) Le style de travail au barrage, qui se situe chez l'un et l'autre sujet à deux régimes de vitesse très différents, correspond bien terme à terme au comportement lexique de chacun.

Disons, pour terminer, que ces deux élèves aux barrages si particuliers, ont été les deux seuls de la classe à ne pouvoir s'y adapter, et ont dû en être retirés.

4ème Partie: étude différentielle des mauvais lecteurs comparés aux débiles, aux détériorés mentaux et aux enfants jeunes.

Les mauvais lecteurs ne sont évidemment pas les seuls à obtenir des résultats défavorables au barrage de signes, aussi avon nous pu confronter nos constatations à celles d'autres chercheurs faites sur d'autres groupes, pathologiques ou non, desquels il était tentant de les rapprocher.

a) — *Mauvais lecteurs et enfants débiles.* (I)

Ils témoignent tous deux d'une inadéquation vitesse-précision (survitesse à B2), mais moins importante chez les M. L. plus inexacts, mais dont la vitesse et le rendement restent voisins de la normale, alors que les débiles sont lents pour leur âge. Les M. L. pratiquant le boustrophédon se rapprocheraient des débiles à B2, quand la tâche devient plus complexe, étant plus rapides qu'eux à BI.

En résumé, comportements assez semblables, mais à un régime plus rapide et moins précis chez les M. L.

b) — *Mauvais lecteurs et sujets adultes ayant subi une détérioration intellectuelle*. (I)

Les détériorés, déjà lents au Ier barrage, réduisent encore leur vitesse au deuxième, quand la tâche devient plus complexe, sans pour cela pouvoir améliorer leur précision. Fatigables, ils sont incapables de maintenir tout au long de l'épreuve un tonus suffisant.

Chez les M. L. on ne trouve généralement pas l'essai d'auto-régulation vitesse: précision tenté, même sans succès, par les détériorés. Les lecteurs pathologiques, lents et imprécis comme ces derniers, ne manifestent pas cette tentative d'ajustement conscient à une tâche plus difficile.

c) — *Mauvais lecteurs et enfants normaux de 6 à 7 ans*. (2)

Les mêmes signes d'imprécision et d'immaturité se manifestent dans les deux groupes, mais très atténués chez les mauvais lecteurs (taux d'erreurs à B2 et fréquence des formules immatures).

Conclusion. Notre échantillon de M. L. ne peut, en tant que tel, être identifié ni aux débiles, ni aux détériorés, ni aux enfants plus jeunes, bien qu'ils se rapprochent des uns ou des autres par telle particularité, et que certains d'entre eux puissent individuellement leur ressembler. Le mauvais lecteur n'est pas, à l'évidence, une entité nosologique.

Conclusion generale

Si les mauvais lecteurs sont à la fois lents et imprécis par rapport à leur âge réel et à leur niveau mental, et peuvent pour la plupart être considérés, lorsqu'ils lisent oralement, comme en survitesse par rapport à leurs possibilités de contrôle de l'exactitude, ils manifestent également des difficultés d'adaptation au niveau de l'exploration visuelle systématisée d'une série de signes graphiques non linguistiques.

Une analyse du style de lecture et du retentissement de l'échec en lecture sur l'ensemble de la scolarité permet de dégager deux types de sujets aux comportements spécifiques à l'épreuve du barrage de signes: les "simples mauvais lecteurs" et les "lecteurs pathologiques".

---

(1) *Enfance* N° spécial sur la débilité: Irène TALAN p. 386—392.
(2) Manuel pour l'examen psychologique de l'enfant (R. ZAZZO) op. cit.

Leurs comportements inadaptés, bien que différents, traduisent également un déficit d'ordre énergétique, lenteur et labilité de la mobilisation, instabilité ou impossibilité de focalisation de l'attention, insuffisance du pouvoir de contrôle, entraînant fatigabilité et désorganisation du comportement, auxquels les garçons paraissent plus sensibles.

Sans exclure les causes possibles d'ordre psychophyiologique (régulation de mouvements oculaires, étendue du champ visuel) ou mnésique (rétention des signes à barrer) une insuffisance de tonus mental, dont l'origine peut-être aussi bien somatique que psychique (I) semble bien caractériser la plupart des mauvais lecteurs, à quoi peut s'ajouter souvent divers déficits linguistiques.

Cet aspect caractéristique de la personnalité des mauvais lecteur nous paraît mérité d'être pris en considération par les maîtres et les rééducateurs dans la choix de leurs méthodes et de leur organisation pédagogiques.

---

(1) R. LEPEZ Psychosociologie de la vie scolaire *Bull. de Psychologie.*
M. GILLY "Bon élève, mauvais élève". Recherche sur les déterminants de la réussite scolaire à condition égales d'intelligence et de milieu social — Thése du Doctorat de 3'cycle Ecole des Hautes Etudes, Paris 1968.

M. D. Vernon

50 CRESSINGHAM ROAD
READING, ENGLAND

The Dyslexic Syndrome and Its Basis

As Money (23) has pointed out, the most striking characteristic of the syndrome in what is sometimes termed "specific" or "developmental" dyslexia is that, in addition to the severe and prolonged backwardness in reading and spelling, there occurs a variety of other symptoms. These are not exclusive to dyslexia; they appear in other cases of backwardness in reading. But there is a characteristic pattern of symptoms, though not all are found in every case of dyslexia. It is, however, useless to attempt to study dyslexia by determining the frequency of distribution of isolated symptoms among the general school population or even among an unselected group of clinic cases. What is necessary is to make a clinical study of each case of marked and prolonged reading backwardness, assessing the occurrence and severity of the symptoms which appear, and thus obtaining a picture of the whole syndrome.

It may then be seen that there are certain symptoms which appear frequently in these cases. This statement does not mean that the symptoms 'cause the Reading difficulty; they may be other consequences of some underlying disability. They, and the reading backwardness, naturally appear with differing degrees of severity. Other symptoms may appear which do not seem to be central to the main disability, though they may aggravate difficulty in learning to read. Such are the environmental factors of poor home background, disinterested parents, and inadequate schooling. Emotional maladjustment is not primary or necessary as a symptom in dyslexia, though frequently emotional disorders arise as its consequence.

But though numerous careful studies have been made of dyslexic children, it then appears that certain symptoms do not always appear and that those which do occur fall into different subgroups within the main syndrome. The question then arises: Is there more than one dyslexic syndrome, and, if so, have the different syndromes different causes?

Two principal types stand out from each other: subjects who appear to be weak in language functions and those in whom the visual analysis of complex shapes is defective. These two types were noted specifically in clinical studies by Ingram (*18*) but have been most clearly distinguished by Kinsbourne and Warrington (*20*). In a set of thirteen severely retarded readers, age eight to fourteen years, the researchers distinguished six cases whose scores on the non-verbal section of the WISC exceeded their verbal scores by at least twenty points and seven cases with the reverse pattern. The first group showed evidence of language impairment: naming and verbal learning were poor, and speech development had been delayed. The second group were particularly poor on the WISC Block Design and Object Assembly tests and at constructional tasks generally; they showed some degree of finger agnosia and were lacking in motor control. They were particularly deficient in the ability for sequential ordering and the manipulation and recall of sequences.

Now it might be suggested that cases of the first type, in which there is frequently clear evidence of early retardation in the acquisition of speech and language functions, are suffering from a form of developmental dysphasia. Although spoken language difficulties may be overcome before school age, there may still be poor auditory discrimination and memory for words. Ingram (*18*) considers that in learning to read these children have particular difficulty in synthesizing phonemes to form the sounds of whole words and sometimes in the comprehension of words.

Kinsbourne and Warrington found that five out of six of their visuospatial cases had histories suggesting birth injury. Several other experimenters have found evidence of the occurence of brain damage in such cases [Statten (*27*), Preston and Schneyer (*24*), and Goldberg et al (*14*)]. The effects of this brain damage sometimes appear in EEG disorders, though not always. Defects in analysis of complex visual forms have often been noted, for instance in the Bender Gestalt test [de Hirsch (*12*), Lachmann (*22*), and Clements and Peters (*9*)] and with the Kohs Block test [Zangwill (*31*)]. Figure-ground and part-whole discrimination may also be inadequate. Some of the most notable features are inability to discriminate between left and right (Cohn *10*) and confusion in the left and right identification of the parts of the body [Benton (*5*) and Belmont and Birch (*4*)]. In addition, there are often hyperkinesis and impulsivity [Clements and Peters (*9*)] and general clumsiness of movement [Kucera et al (*21*)]. Not surprisingly, these cases are very resistant to treatment. Silver and Hagin (*8*) found that twenty-four children followed up over ten years until they were nineteen years old still showed marked reading disability, together with difficulties in figure-ground discrimination and some degree of finger agnosia though left-right discrimination had improved.

However, it cannot be assumed that all cases with visual deficits are suffering from brain damage or that, if there has been any impairment, it is too slight to detect. Moreover, it is known that in many cases a hereditary factor may be involved. Hallgren (*15*) may have overemphasized the frequency of this factor, but there is an obvious number of cases in which other members of the family suffer from reading difficulties and other associated symptoms. Again, other deficits have been noted in dyslexic children which have not been specifically related to brain damage. In some of these, the auditory sense may also be involved, a condition which is significant because many backward readers have particular difficulty in the analysis of speech sounds and their association with printed letter shapes. This difficulty has been found in matching visual and auditory rhythms — the visual being shown in sequences of dots; the auditory, in series of taps. Though Birch and Belmont (6, 7) noted particularly a disability in matching auditory to visual patterns, Beery found that matching visual to auditory patterns was equally poor. It is possible, however, that weak auditory memory for rhythms may have been the important factor. Again, perception of kinaesthetic and tactile patterns may be poor in backward readers with visual deficits [Ayres (1)].

Furthermore, there are cases in which both visuospatial and language impairment are found. And weakness in lateralization, especially of the hands, may appear in many types of cases. But though lack of well-defined laterality has for a long time been associated with dyslexia, some experimenters have found this condition to be of minor significance [Belmont and Birch (4)]. It tends to disappear in older backward readers [Harris (16) and Belmont and Birch (3)]. Tjossem et al (30), however, claim that congenital left laterality may be demonstrated in older backward readers by means of Friedman's test of the position of the "hair-whorl", even though they appear to be right-handed. But directional confusion of some kind may be more persistent and appear in the letter and word reversals which are so characteristic of dyslexics. Nevertheless, even these characteristics tend to disappear in tim.

Now Critchley (11) has attributed all the types of cases described, apart from those suffering from brain damage, to a "maturational lag" in the development of cortical differentiation — hence in achieving the higher levels of visual perceptual function and in establishing visuo-auditory and visual kinaesthetic equivalence. This lag is probably hereditary in origin. There may be a general retardation in neurophysiological development, as shown in slowness to establish cerebral dominance, and to integrate the functions of the two sides of the body [Ayres (1)]. De Hirsch et al (13) have also suggested the existence of a maturational lag appearing in slow differentiation in perceptuo-motor and linguistic performance in the sequencing of auditory events. This condition they have associated with general immaturity of personality, as observed in an infantile method of tackling difficult tasks with inability to respond in a purposeful and organized manner. This behaviour may be compared with the greater impulsivity and poor capacity for analysis noted by Kagan (19) and the greater "field dependence" of backward readers observed by Stuart (29).

Although such a maturational lag may be operating in some dyslexic cases and may be overcome to the extent that reading capacity improves and some of the symptoms described above disappear, nevertheless there are other cases in which reading never becomes really fluent and spelling is always execrable. Moreover, in these cases there appears to be a deficiency in the higher mental processes, especially of concept formation rather than of the perceptual functions. Rabinovitch (25, 26) noted the difficulty in translating percepts into symbols, in the use of conceptual abstractions, and in formulating grammatical sentences. Braun (8) found that backward readers were significantly less able than normal readers to form concepts through abstraction and classification. Moreover, whereas the normal readers improved in this capacity with age, the backward readers showed little or no improvement between the ages of ten and twelve years, indicating that lack of attainment of full facility in reading may be associated with deficiency in forming abstract concepts. Rabinovitch et al (25) suggested that this conceptual deficity may be associated with minor neurological impairment, but Kucera et al (21) found that deficiencies in the higher integrative functions, including difficulties in synthesis and in the understanding of the symbolic significance of graphic signs, were more characteristic of familial cases in which a hereditary factor was indicated.

May one then conclude that within the dyslexic syndrome three main types of cases may be included? The first could be classed as a special type of dysphasia; the second, in which inability to analyse complex visual shapes is the most notable feature, could be attributed to brain damage. This damage might be of a general nature, or it might affect predominantly the parieto-occipital area of the right hemisphere and resemble Gerstmann's syndrome in adult brain-injured cases, as Hermann (17) has suggested. As to the third group, possibly hereditary in origin, with its bewildering variety of symptoms, could it be that there is here a general underlying disability to comprehend and construct complex structures within which are integrated visual symbols in sequential order and other spatial patterns, together with speech sounds (which to the young child may have no recognizable conceptual pattern)? This disability might become focal in immature children in the early stages of word recognition because this is the first difficult conceptual task encountered by the child on entering school. The more mature, however, surmount this stage; but their inherent disability appears at the purely conceptual level, a later stage in learning to read.

REFERENCES

1. Ayres, A. J. "Patterns of Perceptual-Motor Dysfunction in Children", *Perceptual Motor Skills* 20 (1965), 335.
2. Beery, J. W. "Matching of Auditory and Visual Stimuli by Average and Retarded Readers", *Child Development* 38 (1967), 827.
3. Belmont, L., and H. G. Birch. "Lateral Dominance and Right—Left Awareness in Normal Children", *Child Development* 34 (1963), 257.

4. Belmont, L., and H. G. Birch. "Lateral Dominance, Lateral Awareness and Reading Disability", *Child Development* 36 (1965), 57.
5. Benton, A. L. *Right—Left Discrimination and Finger Localization*. New York: Hoeber.
6. Birch, H. G., and L. Belmont. "Auditory-visual Integration in Normal and Retarded Readers", *American Journal of Orthopsychiatry* 34 (1964), 852.
7. Birch, H. G., and L. Belmont. "Auditory-visual Integration, Intelligence, and Reading Ability in School Children", *Perceptual Motor Skills* 20 (1965), 295.
8. Braun, J. S. "Relation Between Concept Formation Ability and Reading Achievement at Three Developmental Levels", *Child Development* 34 (1963), 675.
9. Clements, A. D., and J. E. Peters. "Minimal Brain Dysfunctions in the School Age Child", *Archives of General Psychiatry* 6 (1962), 185.
10. Cohn, R. "Delayed Acquisition of Reading and Writing Abilities in Children", *Archives of Neurology* 4 (1961), 153.
11. Critchley, M. *Developmental Dyslexia*. London: Heinemann, 1964.
12. de Hirsch, K. "Gestalt Psychology as Applied Language Disturbances", *Journal of Nervous and Mental Diseases* (1954), 120, 257.
13. de Hirsch, K. *Predicting Reading Failure*. New York: Harper and Row, 1966.
14. Goldberg, H. K., et al. "The Role of Brain Damage in Congenital Dyslexia", *American Journal of Ophtalmology* 50 (1960), 586.
15. Hallgren, B. "Specific Dyslexia", *Acta Psychiatria et Neurologica*, Suppl. 68, 1950.
16. Harris, A. J. "Lateral Dominance, Directional Confusion and Reading Disability", *Journal of Psychology* 44 (1957), 283.
18. Ingram, T. T. S. "Paediatric Aspects of Specific Developmental Dysphasia, Dyslexia and Dysgraphia", *Cerebral Palsy Bulletin*, No 2 (1960), 254.
17. Hermann, K. *Reading Disability*. Copenhagen: Munksgaard, 1959.
19. Kagan, J. "Reflection-impulsivity and Reading Ability", *Child Development* 36 (1965), 609.
20. Kinsbourne, M., and E. K. Warrington. "Developmental Factors in Reading and Writing Backwardness", *British Journal of Psychology* 54 (1963), 145.
21. Kucera, O., et. al. "Some Observations on Dyslexia in Children in Czechoslovakia", *American Journal of Orthopsychiatry* 33 (1963), 448.
22. Lachmann, F. M. "Perceptual-motor Development in Children Retarded in Reading", *Journal of Consulting and Clinical Psychology* 24 (1960), 427.
23. Money, J. "Dyslexia: A Post-Conference Review", in J. Money (Ed.). *Reading Disability*. Baltimore: John Hopkins Press, 1962.
24. Preston, R. C., and J. W. Schneyer. "The Neurological Background of Severely Retarded Readers", *Journal of Educational Research* 49 (1956), 455.
25. Rabinovitch, R. D., et. al. "A Research Approach to Reading Retardation", in *Research Publications of the Association for Research in Nervous and Mental Disease* 34 (1954), 363.
26. Rabinovitch, R. D. "Dyslexia: Psychiatric Considerations", in J. Money (Ed.), *Reading Disability*. Baltimore: John Hopkins Press, 1962.
27. Statten, T. *American Journal of Psychiatry* (1953), 110, 205.
28. Silver, A. A., and R. A. Hagin. "Specific Reading Disabilities: Follow-up Studies", *American Journal of Orthopsychiatry* 34 (1964), 95.
29. Stuart, I. R. "Perceptual Style and Reading Ability", *Perceptual Motor Skills* 24 (1967), 135.
30. Tjossem, T. D., et. al. "An Investigation of Reading Difficulty in Children", *American Journal of Psychiatry* (1962), 118, 1104.
31. Zangwill, O. L. *Cerebal Dominance and Its Relation to Psychological Function*. Edinburgh: Oliver and Boyd, 1960.

RALPH C. PRESTON

UNIVERSITY OF PENNSYLVANIA
PHILADELPHIA, PENNSYLVANIA
UNITED STATES OF AMERICA

An Appraisal of Medical Research on Dyslexia

MEDICAL CONTRIBUTIONS TO UNDERSTANDING of dyslexia have been numerous and cover ninety years of work. Indeed, members of the medical profession were the first to identify dyslexia as an entity, and it was they who first distinguished it from mental retardation and who pointed out the error in attributing it to laziness on the part of the child or to incompetence on the part of the teacher.

Specialists in the teaching of reading have lagged behind the medical and psychological professions in recognizing the existence of dyslexia. Even today, some reading specialists continue to ignore dyslexia and find uncongenial the concept involved in "typing" a disability. This condition may be due to the fact that educators, unlike medical men, are trained to teach individuals in groups; educators lack the clinical training and, hence, the clinical instincts that would equip them to think of disability in terms of etiology, syndromes, systematic diagnostic procedures, and treatment. The difference in the training and methodology between teachers and medical men, and the validity of both approaches, point to one reason why the teacher and the medical specialist would benefit by familiarizing themselves with the research and insights of the other.

The divergence in research findings and opinion on dyslexia is truly astonishing. The widely differing views can be in part explained by the natural tendency for specialists to confine their reading to journals and books in their own respective fields. The split is not just between education, psychology, and medicine. Within each of these fields the extent of specialization is staggering. There is too little cross-fertilization between the many minds who are working on dyslexia but who approach the problem with diverse assumptions and from diverse angles. It is hoped this paper may make a modest contribution to weakening just one of the barriers — that between education and medicine.

With this purpose in mind, the writer will summarize and evaluate a selection of opinion and findings from the medical literature which typify matters of importance for the teacher of reading and the reading clinician. After the elimination of numerous speculative essays, sources were narrowed to approximately one hundred articles and half a dozen books representing work in fourteen nations. About two-thirds of them appeared between 1963 and 1965, the remainder coming from publications which appeared before and since that period.

The research here reviewed was conducted chiefly by neurologists, psychiatrists, pediatricians, and ophthalmologists. It represents several types of investigation. About one-third of the studies are reports based on clinical experience and impressions; almost as many are diagnostic surveys of children without controls. Next in frequency come diagnostic surveys with controls and cross-sectional clinical studies. Last and too few are reports of longitudinal case histories and autopsies.

Those who believe that anything short of a controlled experimental study is of dubious scientific merit will be disappointed with the dearth of such studies. The writer's own conviction, to the contrary, is that the numerous clinical and observational studies are highly appropriate and necessary in view of the present-day need. This need is for careful clinical observation, followed by theory-building, followed by comparing one's notes with those of others, followed by more observation, followed by more theory-building. Controlled experimentation is more suitable in fields with large bodies of established descriptive material, such as chemistry, or in solving problems related to such matters as respondent behavior. Controlled experimentation in reading has been going on for years, and the few drops of positive knowledge that have been squeezed from it are embarrassingly scanty. Not all the experimental research on reading was necessarily bad, but much of it was premature. Other approaches are obviously called for, including the sort of clinical observation and surveying now being carried out in medicine.

Etiology

There is a distinct tendency today for the cause of dyslexia to be assigned to a disturbed neurologic organization, the most reliable symptom of which is delayed maturation. It is widely accepted that in the true dyslexic there is no history or evidence of brain injury.

Few writers are dogmatic about the precise nature of the dysfunction. Most appear to agree with Rabinovitch (19) who describes dyslexia as "This intriguing but still too mysterious basic etiology . . ." The lack of dogmatism can be further illustrated. Gardner and Sperry (8), for example, although strongly oriented psychiatrically and who regard a reading disability as tied in with an emotional ambivalence which they believe everyone has toward language, do not deny the role of organic factors. Although some psychiatrists contend that their field holds the answers, they are not as uncompromising as Blau (2) in his well-known monograph of twenty years ago. Many today are taking a broader and more objective view. Among these are two psychiatrists, Gerald H. J. Pearson and Herman S. Belmont, with whom the writer has worked in Philadelphia (Preston, in preparation). In a series of eighteen dyslexics, Pearson and Belmont found a larger proportion of weak egos and deficient self-esteem than in a series of controls, but they found negligible differences between the two groups in neurotic symptoms and in need of psychotherapy. They concluded that in only one case did emotional problems alone appear to underlie the reading disability. In nine of the cases, they concluded that subtle organic impairment was fundamental. This kind of detachment that enables a specialist to see causes lying outside his own field is commonplace in medical literature today.

There is a strong presumption that dyslexia is a hereditary disorder. Ingram (15) calls it a recessive trait; Drew (5) and Hallgren (13) call it a dominant trait. Evidence of its being a familial trait has been found in many studies over the years, of which various Scandinavian investigations are frequently cited. Percentages of known familial presence range from sixty-three percent to approximately ninety percent of cases [Hansen (14)]. The belief that dyslexia is a constitutional disorder is strengthened further by the large body of data revealing a higher proportion of male dyslexics than female dyslexics — a proportion of 3:1 to 4:1.

The contemporary medical literature is skeptical of Orton's contention that dyslexia is due to failure of the child to establish unilateral cerebral dominance, a condition accounting for the presence of mixed laterality and reversals, and provides evidence that handedness and eyedness are not reliable indices of cerebral dominance. For example, Goodglass and Quadfasel (12), Penfield and Roberts (17), Goldberg (11), and others have shown that one cannot predict language dominance for left-handed individuals and not perfectly even for right-handed individuals. It is also widely recognized that mixed laterality may be present in cases of normal readers and, moreover, that many dyslexics are free of mixed laterality. But even though the classical theory of cerebral dominance is rejected, the majority of dyslexics are still reported as having some degree of mixed laterality. The mixed laterality is sometimes interpreted as one aspect of the maturational lag found among dyslexics.

It would be an error to suggest that all medical conclusions about the cause of dyslexia are based on evidence. Five reports were examined in which the inconsistent orthography of the English language and the so-called "look-say" method of reading instruction are cited as causal factors. These statements are undocumented and appear to be expressions of mere speculation.

Finally, an interesting point of view by Bender (1) should be mentioned. She believes that the congenital immaturities which lie at the seat of dyslexia may be present in some children but never manifest themselves in the reading process because of the presence of favorable exogenous factors — a favorable emotional climate at home and school, favorable motivation, and favorable opportunities to learn. This is an important point to which the writer will return in discussing treatment.

Diagnosis

It is clear from the literature that the gross neurologic examination (with the possible exception of the EEG about which there is conflicting evidence and judgment) does not reveal diagnostic information about dyslexia. The literature recognizes that subtle types of tests of a variety of functions are required: of laterality, distinguishing right from left, copying of figures, reproduction of block arrangements, taking dictation, drawing, setting the hands of a clock, naming or pointing to individual fingers as directed, and others. Rabinovitch (19) makes a welcome plea against "tests that do not relate to the child's functioning in the life situation" and urges that tests be used that "have meaning in terms of the child's actual real-life learning".

Reading teachers and reading clinicians who examine the medical research literature will be surprised at the general failure of investigators to use the concept of reader level as a supplement to grade- or age- equivalent score or diagnostic instruments such as the informal reading inventories, orally read graded word lists, and oral reading tests. As long as medical specialists stick to rules such as "two years retarded", a net that catches the large numbers of children who are retarded for reasons of cultural and educational deprivation, and as long as they fail to use the diagnostic educational instruments, specialists are going to continue to make exaggerated estimates of the incidence of dyslexia.

A number of medical investigators express proper concern over the loose and extensive use of the concept of "minimal brain damage", popularly inferred from any one of a host of symptoms. It is a medically meaningful term when used appropriately and with restraint, but many writers point out that its present extravagant use is misleading and not helpful diagnostically.

Drew (5), Shankweiler (22), and others emphasize the fact that dyslexia has a variety of syndromes. This point is important. Apart from the reading failure, dyslexic children may be characterized by mixed laterality, inability to discriminate right and left body parts, reversals in their reading and writing, finger agnosia, dyspraxia, abnormal EEGs, and the like. None of these is a constant factor from case to case. Dyslexic children share with one another with certainty only one trait: the gestalt dysfunction revealed by such symptoms as the persistent difficulty in synthesizing word parts, in seeing and building permanent images of word wholes, and in associating sounds with visual symbolization. In study of eighteen dyslexics at the University of Pennsylvania, already referred to, the team neurologist, Martin Mandel, administered fifteen neurological tests mostly of the subtle or "soft" type. The most nearly consistent abnormality was in taking written dictation of simple sentences (all but one case showed dictation abnormalities); next came the EEG (all but three cases showed EEG abnormalities). Each child had his own pattern of symptoms. As Drew (5) concludes, the various inconstant abnormalities reported as characteristics of dyslexia are best viewed as variant manifestations of gestalt dysfunction, perhaps caused by delayed neurologic development.

Incidence

One of the chief blocks to the advancement of knowledge about dyslexia is failure to agree on its characteristics. This omission shows up in the various reports in the literature on the incidence of its occurrence. In the medical literature reviewed, the figures range from two to thirteen percent. Some estimates from other sources have run lower and some higher. The bases of most of the medical estimates are far from satisfactory. Some are not described and seem more like wild guesses. Some are based on hospital populations. Some investigators unfortunately abandon their clinical point of view and uncritically accept school figures of children who are two or more years retarded in reading achievement as indicative of the dyslexic population. It seems that the gathering of data on incidence might better be left to educators and psychologists who are in a better position than physicians to evaluate school tests and school records and who have shown their ability also to use clinical tools as a basis of identifying dyslexic children. The writer suggests as models three comprehensive, systematic surveys by educators who are also clinical psychologists. One was conducted by Stauffer (24) who surveyed the nine- to eleven-year-old population in the Philadelphia public schools and who computed an incidence of dyslexia of one percent. The second was conducted by Schenk-Danzinger (21) who examined 2,000 children in Vienna at the end of their second school year and who obtained a figure of 3.9 percent. The third was conducted by Gaskins (in preparation) of the Reading Clinic of the University of Pennsylvania who included all fourth grade pupils in a small Pennsylvania city and who secured a figure of approximately one percent. It is to be regretted that medical workers, despite their splendid clinical skills and insights, tend to be careless when it comes to estimating the incidence of dyslexia and, as previously mentioned, tend to attach uncritical and undeserved dependence upon the number of years a child is retarded. The result is that some children are placed in the dyslexia category who, if the more rigorous clinical criteria had been applied, would more properly be viewed as nondyslexic retarded readers.

Treatment

Medical reports of results of treatment are few and scattered and are mostly anecdotal. Therapy reported includes psychotherapy administered to the dyslexic, psychotherapy administered to the dyslexic's mother, suggestion, hypnosis, sleep learning, and sedation. Results are generally reported as favorable. Wider experimentation with medical treatment, provided there is systematic evaluation, is to be encouraged.

Most of the writers are content to turn their dyslexic patients over to teachers for treatment and to let the teachers select methods of instruction. A number of medical specialists, on the other hand, have shown little inhibition in expressing their views and prejudices regarding the teaching of reading. Individual tutoring as opposed to group instruction tends to be favored. Some of the methods proposed include use of the rebus device; use of "hieroglyphic" writing, no doubt similar to the German "Sprechspur" [Rahn (20)]; stimulation of the deficit perceptual areas [Silver, Hagin and Hersh (23)], apparently similar to Maney's program (16) and the Fairbanks-Robinson program (6); psychomotor reeducation adapted from the Delacato (4) model; encouragement of the use of the right hand by left-handed dyslexics; the Fernald (7) approach for total or extreme disability; and the Gillingham and Stillman (10) method (more frequently recommended than any other approach).

Rarely do those who recommend special teaching methods reveal knowledge of the research or the pedagogical literature on the subject; and they know apparently little or nothing of alternative approaches to those they propose. The pioneering and promising work of Schenk-Danzinger of Vienna, Tamm of Hamburg, and Norrie of Copenhagen is little known. Botel's hypothesis (3) is still to receive due attention. Botel of the University of Pennsylvania and one of his students, Patricia S. Guth, are testing the proposition that an exemplary school program can prevent the manifestation of dyslexia in most dyslexia-inclined pupils. Their findings to date are impressive and may well demonstrate the truth of Bender's view, previously stated, that the congenital lag that lies at the seat of dyslexia may be present in some children but never manifests itself in the presence of favorable environmental factors. Other work meriting the attention of medical specialists is Willson's important finding (25) that there appear to be at least three identifiable syndrome patterns each of which calls for a unique instructional approach.

Everyone is saying these days that more of the research on dyslexia should be carried out by interdisciplinary teams. Despite the multiplicity of isolated work which the writer has been reporting, influential leaders in medicine and education are taking firm and long steps in the direction of the team approach. As interdisciplinary study advances, the gulf in thinking about dyslexia which today separates medicine and education will begin to disappear.

REFERENCES

(Note: Most of the literature on which this paper is based comprises a part of a larger bibliography which has been compiled and annotated by Jane Levine, research associate, Reading Clinic, University of Pennsylvania, and will form a part of a "state of the art" publication now in preparation by Morton Botel, University of Pennsylvania and commissioned by ERIC/CRIER, a national clearinghouse for materials on reading, Indiana University, Bloomington, Indiana 47401. For other bibliographies, see another ERIC/CRIER publication, *A Citation Bibliography of Selected Sources on Dyslexia and Learning Disabilities* (no annotation); and *Selected Annotated Bibliography: Technical Articles on Dyslexia 1960—1967* prepared by National Institute of Neurological Diseases and Blindness, Bethesda, Maryland, June 1967.)

1. Bender, L. "Neuropsychiatric Disturbances", in A. H. Keeney and V. T. Keeney (Eds.) *Dyslexia: Diagnosis and Treatment of Reading Disorders.* St. Louis: Morby, 1968, 42—48.
2. Blau, A. *The Master Hand.* New York: American Orthopsychiatric Association, 1946.
3. Botel, M. "Methods and Systems for Teaching Dyslexic Pupils", in A. H. Keeney and V. T. Keeney (Eds.), *Dyslexia: Diagnosis and Treatment of Reading Disorders.* St. Louis: Mosby, 1968, 120—130.
4. Delacato, C. H. *Diagnosis and Treatment of Speech and Reading Problems.* Springfield, Illinois: Thomas, 1963.
5. Drew, A. L. "Neurological Appraisal of Familial Congenital Word-Blindness." *Brain,* 79 (1956), 440—460.
6. Fairbanks, J. and J. Robinson. *Perceptual Motor Development.* Boston: Teaching Resources, 1967.
7. Fernald, G. M. *Remedial Techniques in Basic School Subjects.* New York: McGraw —Hill, 1943.
8. Gardner, G. E., and B. Sperry. "Basic Word Ambivalence and Learning Disabilities in Childhood and Adolescence." *American Journal of Psychotherapy,* 18 (1964), 377—392.
9. Gaskins, I. W. "Incidence of Dyslexia." (In preparation.)
10. Gillingham, A., and B. W. Stillman. *Remedial Training for Children with Specific Disability in Reading, Spelling, and Penmanship* (7th ed.). Cambridge, Massachusetts: Educators Publishing Service, 1965.
11. Goldberg, H. K. "Vision, Perception and Related Facts in Dyslexia", in A. H. Keeney and V. T. Keeney (Eds.). *Dyslexia: Diagnosis and Treatment of Reading Disorders.* St. Louis: Mosby, 1968, Ch. 10.
12. Goodglass, H., and F. A. Quadfasel. "Language Laterality in Left-handed Aphasias." *Brain,* 77 (1954), 521—548.
13. Hallgren, B. "Specific Dyslexia ('Congenital Word-Blindness'): A Clinical and Genetic Study." *Acta Psychiatrica et Neurologica* (renamed *Acta Psychiatrica Scandinavica),* Supplement 65, 1950.
14. Hansen, E. "Recent Studies of Dyslexia", *Developmental Medicine and Child Neurology,* 7 (1965), 574—575.
15. Ingram, T. T. S. "Specific Learning Difficulties in Childhood." *Public Health* 79 (1965), 70—80.
16. Maney, E. S. *Reading Readiness Program.* Elizabethtown, Pennsylvania: Continental, 1958.
17. Penfield, W., and L. Roberts. *Speech and Brain Mechanisms.* Princeton University Press, 1959, Ch. 6.
18. Preston, R. C. "Interdisciplinary Study of Eighteen Dyslexics." (In preparation.)
19. Rabinovitch, R. D. "Reading Problems in Children: Definitions and Classifications", in A. H. Keeney and V. T. Keeney (Eds.), *Dyslexia: Diagnosis and Treatment of Reading Disorders.* St. Louis: Mosby, 1968, Ch. 1.
20. Rahn, G. *Handbuch der Sprechspur.* Bohum: Kamp, 1952.
21. Schenk-Danzinger, L. *Studien ur Entwicklungspsychologie und zur Praxis der Schul- und Bertatungspsychologie.* Basel: Reinhardt, 1963, 174—188.

22. Shankweiler, D. "Study of Developmental Dyslexia." *Neuropsychologia,* 1 (1964), 267—286.
23. Silver, A. A., R. A. Hagin, and M. F. Hersh. "Reading Disability: Teaching Through Stimulation of Deficit Perceptual Areas." *American Journal of Orthopsychiatry,* 37 (1967), 744—752.
24. Stauffer, R. G. "Certain Psychological Manifestations of Retarded Readers", *Journal of Educational Research,* 41 (1948), 436—452.
25. Willson, M. F. "Clinical Teaching and Dyslexia", *Reading Teacher,* 21 (May 1968), 730—733.

GRACE WALBY

CHILD GUIDANCE CLINIC
WINNIPEG, MANITOBA
CANADA

Classroom Techniques for the Identification of Retarded Readers

THE RETARDED READER IS THE CHILD who is not reading so well as might be expected in terms of his intellectual capacity to the extent that his school progress is impeded. Because he has had so little success in school, he is apt to be discouraged, disheartened, defeated. He may well have developed negative attitudes towards reading and perhaps towards school in general. The task in planning for him is therefore twofold: to provide the kind of learning experiences that are appropriate for his present level of achievement and to stimulate his interest and enthusiasm for reading as well as growth in skills so that he may in the future achieve at a level more appropriate for one of his ability. In order to achieve these ends it is essential for the teacher to know not only the sequence of skills in reading but also to know the child, *his* needs, *his* interests, and *his* attitudes. Therefore, this paper is directed toward the steps a teacher may undertake in order to identify the needs of the retarded reader.

Once the retarded reader has been identified through a comparison of his achievement in reading with some measure of intellectual ability, there are four questions that will guide the teacher in his search for a solution of the problem. The most important question to answer about a child's reading is, according to Harris (2): "How difficult a book can this child read?" Further insight can be gained through answers to the following: What skills, necessary for efficient reading, has he not yet developed? Are there inhibiting factors, physical or emotional, which can be corrected or which must be taken into consideration in planning his program? What interest can be discovered upon which to build?

How difficult a book can the child read?

In attempting to answer this question it is useful to recall the concepts of the independent, instructional, and frustration levels suggested by Betts (1). The independent level is the highest level at which the child can read fluently. This point is usually determined by the level at which the child makes no more than five significant errors per 100 words. The instructional level is the highest level at which a child can read satisfactorily with teacher guidance and preparation. The frustration level is the level at which a child's reading skills break down, fluency disappears, word recognition errors are numerous, comprehension becomes faulty and signs of stress become apparent.

The most productive means of establishing these levels of reading is through the use of an informal reading test devised by the teacher through the choice of appropriate paragraphs from a series of graded readers. The selections should begin with a paragraph just below the level at which the teacher estimates that the child should be able to read and continue upward until too challenging materials are presented. Provision should be made for upward or downward revision of this scale, as necessary. At this point in testing it is most often extremely productive if the child is taken into one's confidence as to the purpose of this undertaking. If this evaluation can become a collaborative venture in which the teacher and child together attempt to assess the child's strengths and weaknesses in reading, changes in attitude and motivation of the child may be begun.

Standardized silent reading test scores usually indicate the instructional level. However, caution must be used in this interpretation, particularly with retarded readers. Because a child who is a poor reader tends to guess more than does a good reader, the score may overestimate his instructional level. On the other hand, because of his poor attitudes towards reading or because of a poor opinion of himself, he may respond erratically or may fail to attempt many questions. In such cases the score will likely underestimate the instructional level. Therefore, findings from such tests should be verified from estimates obtained through the use of informal reading inventories. Discrepancies between these two estimates point to the need for further investigation.

What skills have not yet been developed?

A pattern of difficulties suggesting possible answers to the second question will begin to emerge as the teacher analyzes the kinds of errors made on the informal and standardized tests. He may note, for example, the child's fluency, expressiveness, and articulation, the extent and success of his use of context clues, the adequacy of his sight vocabulary, his method of attacking new words, and the extent to which he makes use of word analysis techniques. From the child's performance on the silent reading tests, the teacher may note whether there is a consistent pattern to the errors made: the child's attention to detail, his ability to find the main idea and to make inferences, the adequacy of his vocabulary, and his understanding of changes in word meaning according to context. From an examination of test responses, it is also possible to estimate whether his reading is accurate but slow, rapid but inaccurate, or both slow and inaccurate.

From the clues found in this analysis of errors, areas for further investigation can be identified. A check list of the essential reading skills can be developed from an examination of the guide book of the reading series being used. By checking the information gathered against such a check list, the major areas of weakness can readily be determined. It will be necessary to investigate more completely one or more of these areas. If, for example, the main difficulty is in word recognition, it would be helpful to know if the child can discriminate between similar sounds he hears and between similar shapes he sees; if he knows the letters of the alphabet, the sounds of the consonants and vowels, and rules governing variations in sounds; and if he can apply this knowledge in words of one syllable and more. Further, it should be established whether this knowledge has become so well established that the child makes use of his knowledge in analyzing unknown words and whether he makes use of context to verify his attempts to analyze a word. Individual assignments appear to provide the best opportunities for assessment of the area of word recognition.

Probably the best way to explore comprehension is to prepare lessons which require the use of the particular skill the teacher wishes to test. Care must be taken to use material of an appropriate level of difficulty so that problems of vocabulary or word recognition will not impede adequate testing of comprehension.

What are the inhibiting factors?

In enumerating the factors that may impede progress in reading, Robinson (3) lists school practices, emotional disturbances, family and peer relationships, visual difficulties, dominance, brain damage, hearing, and general physical or health problems. Many of these factors stem from outside the classroom; and for such, the teacher's task is one of observation to note symptoms of difficulty, of suggestion to parents or appropriate school personnel of the need for examination, and of provision within the classroom of whatever adjustment is possible to alleviate the difficulty. However, there are often factors which have arisen from the child's lack of success in school and which seem to be impeding further progress. These factors may be noted in the child's reactions to the reading tasks he is given. Does he push the book away or otherwise show his distaste for the tasks? Does he withdraw from the task by daydreaming or superficial efforts? Does he cloak his fear of the task by clowning or assuming an "I don't care" attitude? Has he been so defeated by his frustrating school experiences that a feeling of hopelessness and apathy marks his minimal efforts to read? Is he so anxious that a panic reaction seems to set in when he encounters an unfamiliar word, resulting in wild guessing or over caution in his attempts? Observation of such reactions will lead the teacher to an understanding of the child's feelings and ability to cope with frustrating situations. If the teacher can encourage the child to become involved in a systematic search for his own strengths and weaknesses, changes in attitude from apathy or resistance to a more positive interest may be engendered. In this respect, much depends on the sensitivity and attitude of the teacher.

Interests upon which to build

The importance of discovering and using the interest of the child cannot be gainsaid. The right book at the right time has often proved a powerful incentive in creating a desire to read. Caution must be exercised in depending solely upon expressed interests — these being at times merely an expression of what the child thinks is acceptable to the teacher. One of the simplest, yet most effective ways to discover a child's interests is to watch his daily behavior, his conversation, his drawings, his play — in fact all the activities that encourage his self-expression. Autobiographies have proved useful with older children in eliciting both interests and attitudes. Discovery of interests is a vital part of the analysis of a reading problem because of its implications for the program to be developed.

Concluding statement

The answers to these four questions can provide the framework for an effective program of remedial instruction. Unless the time is taken to discover the specific needs of the retarded reader, the most earnest efforts may be so inappropriate as to cripple him further. It is the teacher's task to do whatever is in his power to help the retarded reader achieve independence and satisfaction in reading. Most children can be helped. When, however, a child is unable to benefit from an intensive, carefully planned program of remediation, further investigation beyond the scope of the classroom is indicated. The teacher's task in such cases is to be sufficiently aware of the special services available in the school system and the community so that he can refer the child for a more extensive exploration of the physical and/or emotional problems impeding progress.

REFERENCES

1. Betts, Emmet A. *Foundations of Reading Instruction.* New York: American Book, 1957.
2. Harris, Albert J. *How to Increase Reading Ability* (4th ed.). New York: Longmans, Green, 1961, 153.
3. Robinson, Helen M. "Corrective and Remedial Instruction", *The Sixtieth Yearbook of the National Society for the Study of Education,* 1961, 362.

Programme Participants Second World Congress on Reading

Copenhagen
August 1—3, 1968

Dr. Oliver S. Andresen
Chicago State College
1450 E. 55th Street
Chicago, Illinois, U.S.A.

M. Gunnar Axberger
Lokevägen 11
Djursholm, Sweden

Professor Richard Bamberger
Director, Children's Juvenile
and Popular Literature
Fuhrmannsgasse 18 a
1080 Vienna 8
Austria

Dr. Franz Biglmaier
1 Berlin 47
Horst-Casper-Steig 29
Germany

Mr. Jan Björnshög
Klockarvägen 5 D
420 11 Hisings-Kärra
Sweden

Mrs. Vera Southgate Booth
School of Education
University of Manchester
Manchester 13, England

Mme. Andrée Girolami-Boulinier
6 rue Voisembert
92 — Issy-les-Moulineaux, France

Mrs. Dorothy Kendall Bracken
3230 Daniel Avenue
Dallas, Texas 75205, U.S.A.

Dr. James I. Brown
Department of Rhetoric
University of Minnesota
St. Paul, Minnesota 55101, U.S.A.

Dr. Chinna Chacko
US AID Education
Rabki Bhavan
Kathmandu, Nepal

Miss Ahalya Chari
Principal
Regional College of Education
Mysore 6, South India

Miss Lutie Chiles
Director of Elementary Education
William Jewell College
Liberty, Missouri 64068, U.S.A.

Miss Claire Chovil
British Broadcasting Corporation
Villiers House
Haven Green
Ealing, W5, England

Dr. Marie M. Clay
The University of Auckland
P.O. Box 2175
Auckland, New Zealand

Dr. Leonard Courtney
St. Mary's College
Winona, Minnesota 55987, U.S.A.

Sister Eileen Marie, Director
Ellen K. Raskob Learning Institute
College of the Holy Names
3500 Mountain Boulevard
Oakland, California 94619, U.S.A.

Mrs. Annie Dahlquist
Nockeby Kyrkväg 48—58
Bromma, Sweden

Dr. Lotte Schenk-Danzinger
University of Innsbruck
Dornbacherstraze 29
A-1170 Wien, Austria

Miss Dorothy Dietrich
Uniondale Public Schools
P.O. Box 105
Uniondale, New York 11553, U.S.A.

Mrs. Ingrid Dobloug
Lillehammer
Norway

Mr. Mogens Ellehammer
Søager 45
2820 Gentofte, Denmark

Mrs. Shoshana Eytan
Director of ULPAN
12 Nathan Strauss Street
Jerusalem, Israel

Dr. Dina Feitelson
The John Dewey School of Education
The Hebrew University of Jerusalem
Jerusalem, Israel

Madame M. Foord
c/o von Toenges
8 etage centre
Number 5, Rue des Grand Portes
1213 Onex
Geneva. Switzerland

Dr. Arthur I. Gates
Language Arts Institute
Teachers College
Columbia University
New York, New York 10027, U.S.A.

Dr. Albert J. Harris
345 E. Grand Street
Mount Vernon, New York 10552, U.S.A.

Mr. Kurt Heidenfors
Kråksätrabacken 19
127 31 Skärholmen
Stockholm, Sweden

Dr. A. Doris Banks Henries
Department of Education
Monrovia, Liberia

Professor Peter Heyer
Pädagogisches Zentrum
Berlin, Germany

Mrs. Alisa Hirsch
Hatibonimstr. 14
Jerusalem, Israel

Dr. Charlotte S. Huck
The Ohio State University
1945 North High Street
Columbus, Ohio 43210, U.S.A.

Dr. Helen Huus
University of Missouri—Kansas City
5100 Rockhill Road
Kansas City, Missouri 64110, U.S.A.

Dr. André Inizan
73 Rue Danielle Casanova
Beaumont sur Oise 95, France

Mrs. Eva Jacobsen
Holsteinsgade 7
Copenhagen, Denmark

Dr. Mogens Jansen
Professor of Psychology
Vejlemosevej 31
Holte, Denmark

Dr. Marion D. Jenkinson
Ontario Institute for Studies in Education
102 Bloor Street West
Toronto 5, Ontario, Canada

Miss Dorothy R. Johnson
Director, Reading Service
Concordia College
Moorhead, Minnesota 56560, U.S.A.

Dr. Mahmoud Roushdi Khater
Arab States Training Centre for Education
for Community Development
Sirs-el-Layyan, Menoufia
Egypt, U.A.R.

Dr. Robert Farrar Kinder
State Department of Education
Box 2219
Hartford, Connecticut 06115, U.S.A.

Dr. Ethel M. King
University of Calgary
3620 6th Street S.W.
Calgary, Alberta 25, Canada

Mademoiselle La Sévre
c/o Dr. André Inizan
73 Rue Danielle Casanova
Beaumont sur Oise 95, France

Mr. Michel Lobrot
248 Rue de Noisy-Le-Sec
93 — Bagnolet, France

Mr. Flemming Lundahl
Anekæret 24
3520 Farum, Denmark

Dr. Sara W. Lundsteen
The University of Texas
Sutton Hall 23 J
Austin, Texas 78712, U.S.A.

Dr. Eve Malmquist
National School of Educational Research
Linköping, Sweden

Miss May F. Marshall
3 Wingfield Avenue
Crawley, Western Australia 6009

Mr. Fergus McBride
Moray House College of Education
Holyrood Road
Edinburgh 8, Scotland

Dr. Constance McCullough
80 Vicente Road
Berkeley, California 94705, U.S.A.

Miss Marjorie J. McLean
Child Guidance Clinic of Greater
Winnipeg
700 Elgin Avenue
Winnipeg 3, Manitoba, Canada

Dr. Amelia Melnik
Reading Development Center
University of Arizona
Tucson, Arizona 85721, U.S.A.

Dr. John E. Merritt
Institute of Education
Old Shire Hall, Old Elvet
University of Durham
Durham City, England

Dr. Ronald W. Mitchell
Assistant Executive Secretary
International Reading Association
Six Tyre Avenue
Newark, Delaware 19711, U.S.A.

Dr. Joyce M. Morris
33, Deena Close
Queens Drive
London, W3, England

Dr. Erik Mortensen
Institute of Educational Technology
Teachers College, Columbia University
525 W. 120th Street
New York, New York 10027, U.S.A.

Professor Heinrich A. Müller
Pädagogische Hochschule
Vechta, Germany

Professor Takeshi Murofushi
Asia University
5 Sakai, Musashino-City
Tokyo, Japan

Dr. Jon Naeslund
Holbergsgatan 129
Bromma, Sweden

Miss Margot Nilson
Stockholms Skoldirektion
Fack 22007
104 22 Stockholm 22, Sweden

M. Claude Philippe
10 Boulevard du Temple
Paris 11, France

M. Jean Piacere
3 rue Adolphe
Cherioux, Issy-Les-Moulineaux 92
France

Dr. Nakorn Pongnoi
37 Sunnalung Road
Chiang Mai, Thailand

Dr. Ralph C. Preston
Graduate School of Education
University of Pennsylvania
Philadelphia, Pa. 19104, U.S.A.

Mr. Gunnar Kjær Rasmussen
Stationsvej 26
Dragør, Denmark

Mr. Anker Ravnmark
4174 Jystrup Midtsj.
Copenhagen, Denmark

Mr. Leif Rigun
Marie Grubbes Alle 22
Lyngby, Denmark

Dr. H. Alan Robinson
Hofstra University
53 Willets Road
Old Westbury, New York 11568, U.S.A.

Dr. Helen M. Robinson
University of Chicago
5835 Kimbark Avenue
Chicago, Illinois 60637, U.S.A.

Dr. John R. Rogers
Director, The Reading Clinic
The University of Mississippi
University, Mississippi 38677, U.S.A.

Miss Ulla-Britt Simm
Swedish Union of Teachers
Trastvägen 9 D, Umeå, Sweden

Dr. Harry Singer
Department of Education
University of California—Riverside
Riverside, California 92502, U.S.A.

Dr. George D. Spache
7221 Sandy Bluff Drive
Jacksonville, Florida 32211, U.S.A.

Mr. G. Srinivasachari
S.I.T.U. Council of Educational Research
3, Thiruvengadam Street
Rajah Annamalaipuram P.O.
Madras 28, India

Dr. Ralph C. Staiger
Executive Secretary-Treasurer
International Reading Association
Six Tyre Avenue
Newark, Delaware 19711, U.S.A.

Dr. Russell G. Stauffer
H. Rodney Sharp Professor of Education
University of Delaware
Newark, Delaware 19711, U.S.A.

Dr. Ruth Strang
Ontario Institute for Studies in Education
102 Bloor Street West
Toronto S. Ontario, Canada

Speciallärare Sture Svensson
Konsertgatan 9
421 39 Västra Frölunda
Sweden

Mr. Karl-Gustav Thorén
Hammarkindsgatan 8
Linköping, Sweden

Dr. Miles A. Tinker
P.O. Box 3193
Santa Barbara, California 93105, U.S.A.

Mr. Ira N. Toff
277 Beverly Road
Scarsdale, New York 10583, U.S.A.

Dr. S. A. Tordrup
Marielystvej 54, F
Copenhagen, Denmark

Miss Ruth Trevor
P.O. Box 12103
Wellington North, New Zealand

Dr. Priscilla Tyler
Stonegate Farm
119th and Metcalf
Stilwell, Kansas 66085, U.S.A.

Dr. Magdalen D. Vernon
50 Cressingham Road
Reading, Berks, England

Mrs. Greta Wahlberg
Bergsprängaregatan 13
412 59 Göteborg, Sweden

Dr. Grace S. Walby
Child Guidance Clinic of Greater
Winnipeg
700 Elgin Avenue
Winnipeg 3, Manitoba, Canada

Dr. Samuel Weintraub
235 Pine Hall
Indiana University
Bloomington, Indiana 47401, U.S.A.

Mrs. Roma Wickenden
Elementary Coordinator
Hardin County Department of Education
Court House
Kenton, Ohio 43326, U.S.A.

Mr. Phillip Williams
Educational Psychology
Department of Education
University of College of Swansea
Wales, United Kingdom

Mr. John M. Wiseley
District Senior Inspector of Schools
New Zealand Department of Education
P.O. Box 430
Wanganui, New Zealand